OPPOSITIONAL DEFIANT DISORDER ACTIVITIES

Oppositional Defiant Disorder ACTIVITIES

Use with Kids Ages 6–12

100 Exercises Parents and Kids Can Do Together to
Improve Behavior, Build Self-Esteem, and Foster Connection

LAURA McLAUGHLIN, LPC SUPERVISOR, RPT

ROCKRIDGE
PRESS

First Rockridge Press trade paperback edition 2022

Rockridge Press and the Rockridge Press logo are trademarks or registered trademarks of Callisto Media Inc. and/or its affiliates in the United States and other countries and may not be used without written permission.

For general information on our other products and services, please contact our Customer Care Department within the United States at (866) 744-2665, or outside the United States at (510) 253-0500.

Paperback ISBN: 978-1-63878-671-9 | eBook ISBN: 978-1-68539-216-1

Manufactured in the United States of America

Interior and Cover Designer: Helen Bruno
Art Producer: Samantha Ulban
Editor: Chloe Moffett
Production Editor: Dylan Julian
Production Manager: Holly Haydash

All images used under license © Shutterstock. Author photo courtesy of Grant Miller Photography

10 9 8 7 6 5 4 3 2 1 0

Contents

Introduction

Let's talk about oppositional defiant disorder (ODD). An array of negative conceptions typically come to mind when someone utters the word "oppositional" or "defiant," and children with these classifications are also often called challenging, extreme, or stubborn. Although this is sometimes true (for all children!), it does not capture the potential within independent, strong-willed, or determined children.

We know that all behavior is goal-driven; however, children with ODD use more maladaptive behaviors to get their needs met. By targeting activities for you and your child to complete and practice together, you will be learning skills to model and teach your child more prosocial and adaptive ways to get their needs met.

I am a child and adolescent counselor. I have worked with many children across the developmental spectrum with an emphasis on treating children with extreme emotional regulation concerns and behavioral meltdowns. Through my work in private practice, I have observed a constant struggle for parents to understand the appropriate way to connect with their children and teach skills related to de-escalation and problem-solving without engaging in conflict and power struggles. This workbook aims to do just that by focusing on activities you can do with your child to teach and reinforce these essential skills. By using your parent–child relationship as the medium for the activities, you are able to tap into the most important and healing mechanism for any child with disruptive behaviors—a positive and affirming connection with you, the parent or caregiver.

Although this workbook is a great resource to help foster a positive parent–child relationship and grow your child's skills of problem-solving and self-regulation, it is not meant to be a replacement for therapeutic treatment or other clinical interventions. This workbook is meant to be an addition to any treatment protocol your family may be engaged in and an extra resource to build your skills at home outside your child's clinical session time with their therapist.

Parenting a child with ODD can be tough, but with the help of the activities in this workbook, I hope that the tough days become few and far between and that your relationship with your child and positive connection will become the primary focus. With the right treatment and dedication to growing skills, it is possible for ODD to be a transient childhood diagnosis and for your child to overcome it and reach their full potential.

How to Use This Book

Chapter 1 provides foundational information about oppositional defiant disorder (ODD) and discusses the related challenges in the child's environment as well as the benefits of the workbook activities. Following that, chapters 2 through 6 each provide twenty activities targeting specific categories of skills for children with ODD.

The activities are meant to be completed by both you and your child together to give you the opportunity to model the skills and to have regular positive interactions with your child. The secondary goal of working on these activities together is to give you the shared goal of completing them and developing a sense of accomplishment, thereby fostering a positive connection in your parent–child relationship. Working together also provides you with a consistent language to use together, and you will be able to cue your child when opportunities arise to practice integrating these skills into their daily life.

These activities are meant to be completed during moments of calm—not in the midst of a conflict or immediately after one. Skills are best grown and developed when a child's brain is open and engaged, and this does not happen during a power struggle or an escalated state. When practicing and referencing these skills, refer to them in a positive manner as opposed to a punitive one. Engaging in these skills should never be a punishment or consequence but a positive opportunity to pause and engage in self-calming, connection, and/or problem-solving.

This workbook is intended to be used in sequential order, but you are welcome to start with any chapter that speaks to you the most or reflects your child's greatest need. That said, do start at the beginning of the chapter because the activities build upon one another as the skills are practiced and integrated.

As a general rule, most of the activities can be completed within fifteen to twenty minutes or less. Using the workbook is a great way to incorporate planned and structured skill-building time daily with your child until the activities are completed.

Most of the activities are intended to be completed with one parent and one child with a few adaptations for additional family members to join in. Once you have practiced these skills with your child, you can generalize them for the whole family and provide your child with ODD the opportunity to positively model these new fun family activities or games for others.

CHAPTER ONE

Getting Started with ODD Activities

RAISING A CHILD who has been diagnosed with oppositional defiant disorder (ODD) can be challenging, and many parents feel overwhelmed and often ill-equipped to respond to their child in a positive manner. This workbook provides activities and techniques that can help you help your child learn to identify and manage feelings that lead to oppositional and defiant behaviors, de-escalate behavior, communicate productively, engage in self-calming, and strengthen your parent–child bond to bring back some peace and cooperation to your home.

In this chapter, you will learn more about what ODD is and get an overview of the activities, which are designed to target the main behavioral symptoms of ODD and foster a more positive relationship with your child.

What Is Oppositional Defiant Disorder?

Oppositional defiant disorder is defined by *The Diagnostic and Statistical Manual of Mental Disorders*, Fifth Edition, as a pattern of angry or irritable mood, argumentative and defiant behavior, and vindictiveness. For a child to be diagnosed with ODD, the problematic behaviors must be consistent for at least six months and be clinically significant compared to other children and typical childhood behaviors for that child's age group. In other words, the disruptive, defiant, and oppositional behaviors are more persistent and frequent than would be expected for a child in that age group and developmental category.

An additional criterion for ODD is that the behaviors must be significant enough to be causing distress to the child and significant others such as family members, peers, or school personnel. This distress must then demonstrate a negative impact on social, emotional, or other important areas of functioning.

In my clinical practice, I often view ODD as the outer behavioral manifestation of symptoms that hint at a larger picture. Although ODD can be given as an independent diagnosis, many children diagnosed with ODD have other mental health conditions such as attention deficit and hyperactivity disorder (ADHD), anxiety, depression, autism spectrum disorders, sensory processing disorders, and/or a history of trauma. It is important to consult with your child's medical providers to ensure that each of the other common co-occurring conditions with ODD have been explored to ensure that your child's treatment is targeting any underlying conditions leading to the outer manifestation of defiant and oppositional behavior.

How ODD Affects Your Child

ODD may manifest in many ways, typically starting with disruptive behavior at home in the parent–child relationship. This is often the initial source of concern. Children often feel the safest and are able to be more vulnerable with their parents, resulting in less restraint or inhibition on disruptive behaviors at home. This usually presents as argumentative behavior, defiance, yelling, aggression, and sometimes violence.

Many children with ODD have emotional responses that seem out of context with the situation at hand. For instance, it is common for a child with ODD to completely lose their ability to function or manage emotions with any slight correction of their behavior. Children without ODD may resist or attempt to negotiate, but a child with ODD often quickly becomes agitated and does everything they can to avoid following directives. This can lead to parents constantly feeling as if they are walking on eggshells (afraid to say or do the "wrong" thing) or that the power dynamics in the house have been reversed and the whole family is at the mercy of the child's unregulated emotions and extreme meltdowns.

Emotional Effects

Children with ODD can be prone to extreme or disruptive emotions that create conflict and tension for the entire household. Children with ODD regularly display feelings of anger and irritation that can quickly turn into violence and aggression without much warning. Sometimes they are able to de-escalate their emotions and manage throughout the rest of the day, but other times, these big emotions may endure and have significant collateral damage for everyone around.

Moderate emotional meltdowns tend to occur at least a few times per day, with the longer meltdowns occurring roughly once per day and lasting a half hour or longer. These meltdowns tend to take a toll on the emotions of parents just as much as the child, creating a perpetual negative emotional tone in the home.

Academic Effects

ODD behaviors that have taken root at home tend to spill over to school and affect the child's academic functioning. Children with ODD struggle to go with the flow and question every directive they are given. Typically, a child with ODD may refuse to follow a teacher's prompt if they do not agree with the request.

The child may misinterpret constructive criticism as a personal attack, leading them to respond in increased oppositional behavior in an attempt to regain a sense of control or power. This can cause the perception of constantly being targeted by school staff and administration, resulting in the child feeling less motivated or cooperative as they do not feel accepted or valued by teachers. The child's perceived lack of acceptance and respect can lead to frequent defiant behavior with the child regularly being punished and ultimately missing intended learning opportunities.

Social Effects

Children with ODD typically struggle in social relationships, as they do not have the adaptability to get along well with their peers. When confronted by peers, a child with ODD is often unwilling to compromise and either attempts to dictate and control the play at all costs or avoids interactions with others completely. This difficulty connecting often leads to them being excluded from social groups and events, creating an even larger gap in the child's social development. This can result in children who are so desperate for peer approval that they go overboard in seeking attention and engage in behaviors that can be off-putting to peers.

Parenting a Child with ODD Is Difficult

Any parent of a child diagnosed with ODD would agree that parenting a child with this disorder is challenging, and many days are filled with counting down the minutes until bedtime so everyone can try again the next day. Many parents feel so overwhelmed and exhausted that they may begin to wonder what led their child astray—and if they had a part in it.

Feeling frustrated or angry at your child's defiant and oppositional behavior is *normal*. It is your brain's biological job to react to an aggressor, even when your child is the aggressor. Parents of children with ODD are constantly working to override their brains' evolutionary response to a threat and respond with calmness and empathy instead. This takes time and practice to learn, and every parent struggles with this—even when their child does not have ODD.

Rest assured, there is nothing you did that caused your child to develop ODD. Children are born with their own temperament and personality, as well as a whole set of biological factors and predispositions to developing certain mental health disorders or emotional responses and ways of being. You are not alone; many parents are struggling with how to respond to a child with ODD. We are all doing the best we can with the skills we currently possess; this workbook will help you gain more.

When to Seek Additional Help

When you first begin incorporating many of the activities and skills outlined in this workbook, the hope is that you notice significant improvement in your relationship with your child, reduced defiance and opposition, increased self-esteem, and an overall increase in your child's ability to manage their emotions.

Some parents may still feel that their child's behavior is out of control and that these activities just aren't quite cutting it. These activities are not meant to replace therapy or other treatment for your child; they are meant to be used in conjunction with your child's other therapeutic treatments or any additional parent–child work you may be doing with a professional.

If your child continues to act out in defiance or anger and is not responding to the activities in this book, or if your child demonstrates any violent or physically

Pause before You React

Children with ODD tend to become immediately escalated when reacting to specific triggers, environmental directives, or cues. Due to brain chemistry and recent research on a phenomenon known as mirror neurons, we now know that our brains want to mirror each other. This means that when your child is escalated, their brain's number one job becomes to make others around them feel the same thing and be just as agitated as they are. This is why children are so good at pushing your buttons when they are angry!

Because children with ODD are so regularly escalated, many parents find that they are often escalated as well and frequently lose their tempers when responding to their child. What this means is that both brains are now escalated and matching each other, leaving no one able to de-escalate the situation. Although this response is natural and what your brain is wired to do, it tends to perpetuate the cycle of reactivity and cause further distress.

This workbook will help you and your child learn the skills to de-escalate and take a pause before reacting so that you can use mirror neurons to your advantage. When you are able to pause and use self-calming skills before responding, you are providing a sense of calm your child's brain will match, leading to de-escalated emotions from all involved. Quick skills such as taking a few deep breaths or walking away for a moment and returning once you have cooled down make a big difference in reducing the level of reactivity.

aggressive behavior during meltdowns and tantrums, then seeking additional help from a licensed mental health provider or medical doctor is recommended. Psychologists, counselors, therapists, and pediatricians can help with assessments and parent interviews to determine if your child may have ODD and work with you to determine the best treatment path to your child's success. There is no reason to feel alone in this work; mental health providers specializing in ODD can help reduce parental feelings of shame or guilt, model and teach effective coping skills to your child, and help restore peace in your home.

How the Activities Can Help Your Child and Improve Your Relationship

As you work through these activities, you will likely begin to notice that your relationship with your child is improving along with your patience and tolerance for misbehavior. In turn, your child will likely feel this greater sense of connection and validation from you, which can potentially turn on their brain to behaving in ways that increase this sense of connection and attachment. Practicing these activities is meant to decrease negative behavior because your child will be seeking your attention and connection in a more positive way.

Children with ODD typically struggle with correctly identifying their feelings, appropriate communication, emotional regulation and self-control, and problem-solving; they also tend to have lower self-esteem. This workbook focuses on these areas to help your child with ODD develop better coping skills to manage emotions and behavior, keep escalated behavior to a minimum, and build better connections with you.

Framing these activities as fun exercises to do together can help with your child's willingness, but you may initially need additional rules or incentives to get active participation, such as requiring two activities to be completed together before screen time is allowed. I recommend initially doing these activities when you and your child are in a good mood, and later on, as these activities are practiced and strengthened, specific activities can be used during a conflict or when you are struggling to connect. The desired goal is for your child to feel the positive impact of these activities, increasing their motivation and desire to engage.

Identifying Feelings

To be able to control their behaviors, children must be able to correctly identify their feelings. We all must be aware of emotional sensations we are experiencing if we want any chance to manage that emotion properly. Being able to identify feelings is a critical first step in improving behavior and simply cannot be overlooked. The activities in chapter 2 focus on increasing your child's feelings vocabulary, get your child more comfortable talking about vulnerable feelings, and begin to tap into the more advanced skills of empathy and perspective-taking by being able to sense what others are feeling.

Communicating Instead of Acting Out

Once your child is able to practice identifying their feelings, chapter 3 focuses on appropriate ways to communicate those feelings to others. Effective communication requires skills related to expressive and receptive communication. Activities centered on expressive communication focus on increasing your child's ability to communicate their needs clearly and succinctly in a positive way. Some activities focus on improving receptive communication, or the skill of active listening. Being able to appropriately communicate their emotions and then using receptive communication to correctly hear validation and redirection from others helps significantly reduce destructive ODD behaviors and leads to the next skill of self-regulation.

Practicing Self-Control and Returning to Calm

One of the most challenging skills for a child with ODD is self-regulation, otherwise known as self-control. These children tend to become escalated and lose control of their bodies and emotions immediately and do not seem to have the ability to take a pause and engage in restraint when they become angry or stop the spiral of destructive behavior once it begins.

Chapter 4 targets the skill of self-control and the ability to de-escalate situations before they get out of hand by distracting the brain from the problem and focusing energy and attention on controlled breathing and calming or self-regulating behaviors.

Solving Problems before They Get Out of Hand

Children with ODD often have a more difficult time with problem-solving because of their emotional reactivity and tendency to act impulsively (whether related to co-occurring ADHD or not). Chapter 5 focuses on engaging the frontal cortex of the brain to strengthen the executive functioning skills necessary to be able to take a pause and problem solve before reacting. The brain is like any other organ—it needs to be fired to be wired, or if you are a workout junkie, you know the similar term "use it or lose it." Activities in this chapter are like dumbbell curls for your child's brain.

Building Connections and Self-Esteem

Many children with ODD have low self-esteem and low self-worth because they are often in trouble. They commonly internalize negative messages about themselves when they are scolded, and this negative mindset perpetuates the spiral of oppositional and defiant externalized behavior. Chapter 6 aims at strengthening the parent–child bond, increasing your child's self-esteem, and creating a positive connection between you and your child. As your child works on these activities with you and has repetitive experiences of connection and acceptance from you, their behavior and your parent–child relationship will likely improve.

How to Approach These Exercises

Throughout this book, I will be outlining activities that can be useful with children diagnosed with oppositional defiant disorder, or any child with defiance towards following rules and limits set by others. By nature, because they are inherently strong-willed and independent children, they are the least likely to be adaptive or willingly participate in new activities presented by parents—especially if it interferes with their own desires or games they want to play.

I have found that a little creativity in how the activities are presented can go a long way. I also recommend you do not suggest these activities in lieu of regular social time with friends, video games, or screen time. If a child has an expectation that they will have those options and you try to force parent-child bonding time, the plan is likely to backfire. Certain children may also need downtime to relax after completing homework to give their brain a break. If this is the case, let them decompress and then during another calm moment you can attempt to approach your child with excitement about spending time together and doing some fun activities.

It's an Invitation, Not an Order

When suggesting the activities outlined in this book, it is all about how you present them. Phrasing them as fun, special play or games with a caregiver as opposed to a demand or requirement is more likely to get the child to cooperate. As with any request for cooperation, saving these activities for a calm, relaxed moment always helps.

Statements starting with "what about . . ." or "what if today we tried a new activity?" can be helpful. Phrase it as an invitation or a statement of curiosity or wonder, not a direct order. An oppositional or defiant child will immediately resist an order, even for play or something that is supposed to be fun. A suggestion or question, on the other hand, may intrigue them.

Taking cues from your child will be important when first attempting to introduce these activities. Finding a balance between gently challenging your child versus pushing too far—and potentially leading to more oppositional behavior—is key. If your child is currently stressed, irritated, frustrated, or annoyed, do not introduce the activity then. Give everyone some time to cool down and come back to it later when they are in a better headspace. Any invitation, no matter how appealing, will be shot down if the receiver is already in an agitated state.

Keep It Flexible

While the activities in the book include specific numbered instructions, making your child follow a rigid schedule exactly as written may lead to resistance from your child and might be counterproductive in some situations. While the activities are laid out in a progressive order, sometimes giving the child more control by allowing them to choose the activity can be helpful. Allow your child to flip through the book and select the most appealing activity if needed, even if you go way out of order. Every activity aims to grow positive skills, so you can't go wrong with any of them.

Other moments may call for flexibility in how you do the activities. If your child is only able to give 5 minutes of effort at a time when talking about feelings, choose one of the shorter activities, such as Fast Feelings on page 14, and call it a day. Is your child having a difficult day? Jump to page 16 and have them identify their Heart Song and do an activity to cheer them up. Being flexible with these activities will sometimes require effort on your end to pre-select the activity (or chapter) that your child needs the most in that moment.

Responding to Resistance

Knowing that this workbook is targeted toward children with oppositional and defiant tendencies, it is normal for your child to express some resistance. As stated previously, these are new skills your child will be working to grow and strengthen, and learning new things is difficult. It takes sustained effort to master new skills, especially ones related to communication, controlling emotions, problem solving, and—the hardest one—talking about feelings.

When presented with these activities, some children may flat out refuse, while others may engage in the activities with half effort or blow it off and give silly answers. If your child refuses to participate, decide beforehand what alternative choices will be available. It would not be wise to compete against any type of screen time, so you can offer the choice of doing the activity together or having twenty minutes of quiet, independent reading time. You could also use positive reinforcers, such as if your child successfully completes two activities with you, they get an additional fifteen of screen time after all homework is completed. Once your child gets a taste of what the activities are like and how connected and supported they feel after completing them, they will hopefully become more motivated. Resistance should decrease over time.

Take Care of Yourself

Through practicing the activities in this book, your child will hopefully develop skills to more effectively control their emotions and decrease problematic behaviors. A likely additional benefit is that you, the parent, will also improve your own positive communication and emotional identification and processing skills. Completing this workbook can increase your confidence as a parent and in your ability to parent a challenging child.

Throughout this book, please take time to acknowledge your own efforts and work as you move through the activities. Teaching and practicing new skills with your child takes patience, compassion, and empathy. These skills will hopefully help improve your relationship with your child, but nothing is a quick fix. There will be moments (or days) when your child simply cannot handle the challenge of some of the activities and will not have the bandwidth to practice developing new skills. It is okay to give yourself and your child a break when needed. No one ever said you needed to complete the workbook in a certain amount of time! Do your best and acknowledge your own efforts and small gains.

You've Accomplished the First Step

I have found that my clients with ODD often tend to be the most brilliant, creative, and loving children. Although they have many beautiful characteristics, it can some-times feel as if their positive qualities are in the shadows because the challenging behavior is so pervasive and all-encompassing.

Parenting a child with ODD is no doubt challenging, but it can also be very reward-ing. When your child's behavior begins to shift and your patience with them improves as a result of doing the activities and increasing your skills, it is hoped that you will start seeing the light at the end of the tunnel. ODD is not a lifelong disorder but clini-cally is seen as a transient, childhood diagnosis. You will get through this period and you and your child will come out better and stronger on the other side if you are able to work together and use the resources necessary. With this workbook in hand, you have already taken a huge first step in turning things around and restoring peace to your home.

It is important to note that you can only give what you have, so be sure to take time for yourself and practice self-care as you work your way through the activities. Many of them can and should be adapted to use on your own! Giving yourself patience, flexibility, and self-compassion is one of the best things you can model for your child with ODD. Let's get ready to dive in!

CHAPTER TWO

Identifying Feelings

THESE ACTIVITIES FOCUS on the all-important skill of identifying feelings. Being able to correctly identify and articulate feelings is the first necessary step to managing those feelings. If we are not aware of what we are feeling, we will have no idea how to handle it. Through the act of labeling their emotional experience, your child will already have begun to de-escalate their emotional reaction to the triggering event. When we can name an experience, it becomes more manageable. Identifying feelings is not natural to many children, and they tend to deny their feelings or inaccurately label them. Be patient with your child as this skill takes time to grow and nurture.

Fast Feelings

SUPPLIES: TIMER, PEN OR PENCIL, PAPER

This activity is an introduction to talking about feelings with your child to slowly start to grow their tolerance for experiencing emotions. The more you talk about emotions, the less taboo they become and the easier they are to manage. Any talk of emotions can be difficult and takes a lot of energy from your child, so try this out when your child is calm, well fed, and rested.

1. Set the timer for 60 seconds, 90 seconds, or 120 seconds depending on your preference.

2. Thinking quickly, write down as many feeling words as you can in the set time. Think outside the box of feelings you may not think about frequently and let your mind go! Don't worry about spelling.

3. When time is up, trade your list with your partner to count and verify. To be counted, the words must be a real feeling. Whoever wrote down the most feeling words wins!

> PLAY TIP: Dive deeper with this activity by going through your lists of emotions and talking about each one. Making it personal can be difficult when your child is first starting to identify their feelings, so as you go through each feeling word, work together to identify a time when most people would typically experience that feeling. This helps your child start becoming more comfortable with feelings words.

Candy Feelings

SUPPLIES: SMALL CANDIES (SUCH AS M&M'S OR SKITTLES) OR
CEREAL PIECES IN FIVE DIFFERENT COLORS

Not only is this activity focused on feelings, but it's also yummy. Each piece of candy or cereal will represent a feeling to help your child think about these feelings in various situations. The aim of this activity is to identify the many different triggers that cause us to experience various emotions throughout the day.

1. Pour an amount of the candy or cereal that you are okay with your child eating into a bowl to control how much candy is consumed overall.

2. Each player takes a handful of pieces as their portion.

3. Assign each color one of the following feelings: happy, sad, angry, proud, and scared.

4. Take turns picking up a piece of candy and sharing a time you experienced that feeling within the past week. For example, if you chose happy for green, share something that recently made you happy for each green piece.

5. Keep going until you have talked about a feeling for each of your pieces. Then eat and enjoy!

> PLAY TIP: For older kids or those with more experience identifying feelings, you can make the activity more challenging by choosing more complex feeling words such as *guilty*, *confident*, or *embarrassed*.

Heart Songs

Ever hear a song and just immediately want to dance? Do you have a go-to song when you are in a bad mood and need a pick-me-up? Music has a unique way of reaching our inner emotions. Talking about how a song can change our mood helps your child with emotional awareness and identifying happiness.

1. Ask your child to think for a moment and identify a song that always makes them feel happy or puts them in a good mood when it comes on. Tell your child, "This is your Heart Song! A Heart Song is a song that makes you feel happy in your heart and warms your soul."

2. Discuss with your child why this song makes them feel happy. Here are some questions to ask:

    *   Are you drawn to the lyrics? Or the beat and musical sounds?

    *   Does the song bring to mind a particular memory of a person or place that makes you happy?

    *   How do you know you are happy when you listen to this song? What does your body do?

3. Play the song and listen together.

4. Get up and dance—it's optional but encouraged!

5. Switch roles. Now it's your turn to identify and talk about your favorite song and listen to the song together.

> **PLAY TIP:** Create a fun way to come back to each person's Heart Song and remember to play the songs when you each need a pick-me-up. Scheduling family dance parties is a perfect opportunity to play these songs and help your child continue to identify what makes them happy.

Feelin' Blue

SUPPLIES: PAPER; BLUE CRAYONS, PENCILS, OR MARKERS

Everyone feels sad from time to time, and many of us have days when we just feel blue. It is very normal to have these days, but many children think there is something wrong or bad about feeling sad. This activity normalizes this emotion and helps teach that sadness is okay, especially when something really sad happens.

1. Take turns thinking of something sad that happened recently. Share this memory with each other and talk about why it made you sad. Be sure to include all the details:

   - How did you know you felt sad in this memory?

   - How do you feel right now when talking about it?

   - What happened in the moments after the sad memory, later that day, later that week, or a few weeks after (if it was a big incident)?

2. Once you've shared the sad memories, each person draws a picture of their sad memory using a blue writing utensil.

3. When you are done drawing, take turns describing your pictures to each other.

4. Talk with each other about how you had to be brave to make it through this sad memory and about why it is okay to feel sad sometimes.

> PLAY TIP: Negative, uncomfortable, or vulnerable emotions are difficult to talk about, especially for a child with ODD. Taking time to create space for these difficult emotions reduces the intensity of them. It will be tempting to jump right to a solution to take away the sadness, but resist this urge! We must first learn to be okay feeling our emotions before we can learn to manage them.

ABC Feelings

SUPPLIES: PEN OR PENCIL, COLORED PENCILS OR CRAYONS

Now that you have been working through some feeling activities, let's see how creative you can be with naming different emotions. This game helps expand your feelings vocabulary and enables your child to better identify emotions because they will have a more expansive list of feeling words in their mind to choose from.

1. On the next page, work together to write feeling words that begin with the different letters of the alphabet.

2. Try to complete as many as you can, but don't get hung up if you have a hard time with some of the quirky letters. (Hint: I see you being zealous and trying to get them all!)

3. After you've worked on it as a team, decide together if you want to consult a list of feeling words from the internet to help guide you.

4. Once you have written all the feelings, your child can color in the block letters while you talk about all the unique feeling words you chose.

5. Discuss together which letters were most difficult and which ones were easy.

> **PLAY TIP:** You can personalize this activity by doing it with the letters of your names. Or turn it into a connection activity with each person doing the other person's name and listing feeling words that describe how they think the other person feels. Discuss what you listed for each other.

Picture Book Feelings Detective

SUPPLIES: YOUR CHILD'S FAVORITE PICTURE BOOK

This activity is the perfect opportunity to snuggle up with your child and experience their favorite picture book in a whole new way! Using books is a great way to introduce various feelings to your child through the different characters' experiences while building the skills of empathy and perspective taking.

1. Look at the pages of the book together, but do *not* read any of the words. Cover the words with scrap paper if that helps.

2. Try your best to guess what each character on the page is feeling. Use clues from the setting and background to help you out if needed. For example, is something broken or spilled in the background? If so, the character may be feeling guilty or sorry.

3. Keep going through each page, trying to use new feelings words as often as you can. For example, many characters may look happy or calm. Try using some of these additional feeling words to see what fits: "curious," "interested," "bored," "thankful," "attentive," and "excited."

4. After you have played the role of feelings detective, go back to read the book together and see how well the feelings you used match the words on the pages.

> PLAY TIP: This game is more challenging with a book your child has not read yet. Give your child a few warm-up rounds with a familiar book, and then up the ante with a new book. For older children, you can do this activity with comic strips or graphic novels.

Freeze Frame

SUPPLIES: ACCESS TO YOUR CHILD'S FAVORITE SHOW

Turn screen time into a useful feeling-identification game! This is similar to "Picture Book Feelings Detective" but takes it a step further. Being able to recognize feelings in others helps children recognize when they need to adapt their behavior based on facial cues and more accurately evaluate how they are doing in social situations.

1. Find a cozy spot to cuddle up with your child and turn on their favorite TV show.

2. Begin watching the show together and pause every few minutes to discuss the following:

   - Who is the main character on the screen?

   - What feeling is this character having right now? How do you know this character is feeling that way (something they said and/or clues in body language)?

   - Why is the character feeling that way?

3. As the show progresses, pause it to talk about how the feelings change. Use these prompts to guide you:

   - Was there a challenge the characters had to overcome?

   - How did they feel when they were right in the middle of the challenge?

   - If they overcame it, how did they feel afterward? How did you know they felt this way?

4. Continue discussing every few minutes until the show is over.

> PLAY TIP: To add a challenge, watch the show on mute and use only nonverbals (body language and facial expressions) for clues about how the characters are feeling. With older kids, discuss the villain's perspective as well.

Safe Zone

SUPPLIES: PLAY-DOH OR OTHER MALLEABLE DOUGH

Feeling safe is one of the most important emotions for anyone. We all have people, places, or items that can help us feel safe. This activity helps your child identify safe or comforting items to enable them to self-soothe, such as when they are in their room alone at night or away from you.

1. Play with the dough for a few minutes just for fun.

2. Next, while playing with the dough, take turns talking about things that help you feel safe.

   • Is it a person, place, or item?

   • When has this person or item helped you feel safe before?

   • What are some signs that you are feeling safe?

3. Now mold the dough into something that makes you feel safe or something similar or even a part of the safety item. For example, if your dog is your safety item, mold the dough into the shape of your dog. If that seems too difficult, mold the dough into a paw print or even just a tail.

4. Make as many safe things as you want from the dough and share what you are making with the other person.

> PLAY TIP: Sometimes ambiguous feelings, such as feeling safe, are more difficult for younger children to identify. Help them get started by first modeling one of your safety items and giving examples of how you feel safe in your body—for example, calm breathing, relaxed heartbeat, and a gentle smile on your face.

Ocean Storm

SUPPLIES: PAPER; CRAYONS, MARKERS, OR COLORED PENCILS

This activity continues from "Safe Zone" but targets the opposite emotion: fear. Talking about or labeling feelings, also known as externalizing emotions, takes away the power and strength behind the emotion. When we talk about it with a safe person, it immediately makes it feel less scary.

1. Close your eyes (if you feel comfortable) and visualize a storm. Where is the storm taking place? What type of storm is it? Describe how it looks as if you were watching it on TV. Are there any people or animals caught in the storm? If not, where are they? If yes, what is happening to them?

2. Draw a picture of the storm.

3. Identify the emotions someone might be feeling during a storm like the one you drew.

4. Talk about how you can feel safe again after a storm like this and what you would need to make it safely through a big storm.

5. Have there been other times in your life when you felt scared? What was happening? Who or what was there to help you feel safe again?

> PLAY TIP: It is tempting to glaze over talking about things that may elicit fear in your child (such as a big storm), but it is important to give space for these emotions. Try not to rescue your child too quickly. They need to have a way to process and release scary feelings before they can move on from them.

In My Heart

SUPPLIES: CRAYONS OR COLORED PENCILS

It's time to focus on some warm, fuzzy feelings! This is a great activity to do together when your child is having a hard day by placing some attention on things that help your child feel loved. When children feel loved, outward behavior improves, and destructive behavior is greatly reduced—a win-win!

1. Think of all the different things that make you feel loved. Talk about them with the other person. Use the following prompts to help with your discussion:

   - How do you know if you are loved?

   - What is the way you like to show love to others?

   - What is your favorite way of receiving love from others?

   - What types of things give you a warm, fuzzy feeling inside?

2. Write or draw a picture of these things inside the heart on the next page. The second person can draw a heart on a separate piece of paper and use that.

3. Color your heart or the pictures you drew.

PLAY TIP: This activity helps your child begin thinking about their own love language and gives you insight into how your child likes to give and receive love. Love languages are introduced in the well-known book *The Five Love Languages* by Gary Chapman and include giving gifts, physical touch, words of affirmation, acts of kindness, and quality time.

Feeling Mime

SUPPLIES: DRESS-UP CLOTHES OR PROPS (OPTIONAL)

Most of what we say when we communicate with others is communicated nonverbally—through facial expressions, body language, and posture. It's important for children with ODD to be able to accurately interpret the nonverbal language of others so that they can receive proper feedback on how they are behaving. This activity helps children learn to recognize the nonverbal signals present when we are communicating different emotions to others.

1. Decide who will be the "mime" and who will be the "observer" first.

2. The mime chooses a word from the "Feelings List" and acts it out silently. No words or sounds allowed! Really think about being dramatic and animated in your facial expressions and body to show this emotion.

3. The mime can use some props, if desired, to help them act out the feeling word. They can also move around the room. For example, if you choose the emotion "focused," you could grab an item and stare at it really hard. For "tired," you could yawn, grab a blanket, and lie down.

4. The observer watches the mime and tries to guess which feeling the other is acting out.

5. Switch roles so that each person gets to be the mime and the observer for a few rounds.

FEELINGS LIST

Angry	Frustrated	Left out	Scared
Calm	Grumpy	Lonely	Silly
Embarrassed	Guilty	Loved	Stressed
Excited	Happy	Nervous	Surprised
Focused	Hurt	Sad	Tired

PLAY TIP: Using the list provided for the first few rounds can help the observer guess correctly without feeling frustrated. These feeling words have also been intentionally chosen as they are some of the more common ones expressed by children. Once you get the hang of it, feel free to use any other emotions.

Feeling Taboo

SUPPLIES: SCISSORS, PAPER, PEN OR PENCIL

This activity is the opposite of "Feeling Mime." The purpose of this game is to be as descriptive as you can without saying the feeling word or any part of the word. This requires you to think about context and what would make someone feel the feeling, tapping into priceless skills of empathy and perspective taking.

1. Cut a piece of paper into ten medium-size squares.

2. On each square, write one of the following feeling words: "irritated," "shy," "proud," "jealous," "brave," "concerned," "helpless," "worried," "rejected," and "thankful." Fold the squares in half with the words on the inside.

3. Decide who will go first. The first player chooses one of the folded squares. Using full sentences, they describe that feeling to the other player without using the word itself or any part of the word. For example, if you get the word "thankful," you might say something like "It's how you might feel when someone gives you a gift." You would not be able to say, "It's the main feeling on Thanksgiving" because it contains part of the word ("thank").

4. After the word is guessed, switch places, and continue playing until all the words have been used.

> PLAY TIP: The feeling words in this activity were chosen for their level of difficulty. Try them out, but if they are too challenging for your child, you can swap them out for other feeling words. The purpose is to stretch and grow your child's emotional vocabulary.

Emo Jingle

SUPPLIES: PAPER, PEN OR PENCIL, BACKGROUND MUSIC
AND PRETEND MICROPHONE (OPTIONAL)

This activity taps into your child's creative side while also further developing the skills of feeling identification. When we sing something, we tend to remember it better. By singing songs about emotions, you are helping your child remember more feeling words so that they can more accurately label how they are feeling in different situations.

1. Pick your child's favorite song or a current song that has a good tune to use as your jingle.

2. Together, pick a feeling word to focus on. Some common lyrics include emotions like heartbreak, betrayal, jealously, love, happiness, or freedom, but you can choose any emotion.

3. Using the tune of the song and working together, create your own jingle about the feeling and write it down. You can keep some of the song lyrics and just switch out a few key words or come up with something new. You can even write different verses for each person to sing or have one person sing the verse and both sing the chorus together.

4. If you are having trouble coming up with lyrics, think of situations between friends or family members. For example, if you choose to do a jingle about feeling free, you could write something about going on sleepovers, staying up as late as you want, and eating all the junk food you can.

5. Once you have the words, practice singing the jingle together. (Using pretend microphones can be fun here.) Don't worry about your singing voice! All voices are beautiful.

> PLAY TIP: The point of this activity is to be creative and silly. Make-believe songs are easier because you can get even more creative, such as a song about a street dog feeling jealous about a pet dog's nice home.

Feelings Pyramid

SUPPLIES: PAPER, PEN OR PENCIL

In this activity, feelings are arranged based on frequency. Doing this activity helps you see your child's emotional burden, meaning you get to see what feelings your child is carrying around the most and which ones they rarely feel. You may be surprised by the emotions your child identifies as common ones they experience. You may be surprised by your own as well.

1. Draw a big triangle that takes up almost all the space on your paper. Then draw four horizontal lines through your triangle, making different levels in the triangle similar to a food pyramid.

2. Think of the five most common feelings you feel on most days or feelings you feel at least part of the day on most days.

3. Rank the feelings in order from most frequent to least frequent.

4. Now write the feeling that you feel most often each day in the bottom layer of your pyramid. Then write the second most common feeling you feel in the second layer up. Keep going until you have written the feeling you feel the least at the very top in the smallest part of the triangle.

5. Talk with your partner about the feelings you chose and why you ranked them this way.

> PLAY TIP: This activity can be a little challenging for younger children, so you may need to point out some feelings you are observing in them in that moment—for example, "I notice you are calm right now. What spot should that take in your pyramid?" or "I saw you get stressed trying to think of what to write. Maybe stressed is one of your pyramid layers?"

Body Talk

SUPPLIES: CRAYONS OR COLORED PENCILS

Your body has many ways of talking to you and sending you messages about how you are feeling. One of the ways your body communicates to you is through sensations that arise in specific situations. Ever notice the prickly feeling you get when something feels off? Or butterflies in your stomach? Your body is talking to you in many ways—it's now your job to learn how to listen and help your child do the same.

1. Think for a moment about where you feel emotions in your body and discuss. Help your child identify at least five different emotions they feel somewhere in their body. A couple examples include feeling nervous in your chest when it gets tight or scared in your tummy.

2. Assign a color to each of the different feelings identified and create a color key.

3. On the image of the body on the next page, have your child color to show where they feel that emotion in their body. For example, if yellow represents happy and they feel happy in their hands, they would color the hands yellow. If red is for angry and they feel angry in their feet or hands, they would color parts of the feet and hands red. Some people feel different things in the same part of their bodies at different times; that's okay! Body parts can share colors and feelings.

PLAY TIP: This activity helps your child develop greater mind–body awareness. The more aware we are of our feelings, the better we are able to manage them. After this activity, begin modeling when you are listening to your body ("My feet are jittery—I must be excited!") to help your child develop this awareness, too.

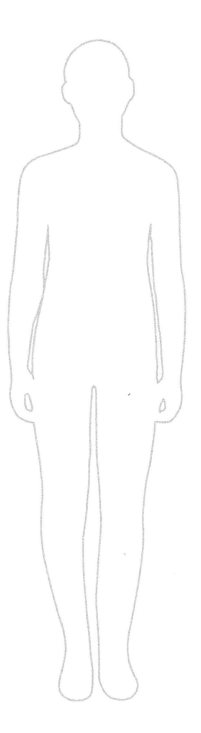

Anger Scribble

SUPPLIES: PAPER, RED CRAYON

Anger gets a bad rap, and most children do not have any idea about what an appropriate way is to express anger or how to release it. This activity helps create a safe space to allow for anger to exist without judgment. No emotion is bad; it's how we respond to and handle that emotion that matters.

1. Think about a situation that makes you angry and share it with the other person. Here are some prompts for help:

   • What part made you the angriest about this situation?

   • How do you feel right now talking about it?

   • How long did you feel angry after this happened?

   • In this situation, how did you show you were angry?

2. While thinking of what makes you angry, grab the crayon in your fist and scribble as hard as you can across the paper. Keep going with your angry scribbles until thinking of the situation makes you not quite as angry or until you feel a little better.

3. See if you can think of a few other situations that made you angry and scribble some more.

PLAY TIP: The point of this activity is to begin talking about anger, so find whatever tactile or concrete representation your child prefers. Most children enjoy making angry scribbles, but crumpling or ripping up the paper works just as well!

Gut Feelings

Our gut tells us a lot about our emotions. One chemical that's associated with mood is serotonin; it's known as the "feel good" chemical because it lifts our mood. Your gut is the largest source of serotonin in your body and houses more of this chemical than your brain! Focusing on gut emotions often helps you identify your most authentic feelings about things.

1. Place both of your hands gently on your gut. This is located in the middle part of your body around your stomach, but you may feel gut sensations a little higher or lower, too.

2. Close your eyes and think about a time you had a gut feeling, or instinct, about something or someone. Your gut was communicating your feelings to you! Share this experience with the other person. Here are some helpful prompts:

   • What does a gut feeling actually feel like, and how do you know it's happening?

   • Why is it important that our bodies communicate things to us about new or different situations?

3. Think of situations when your gut might warn you about danger or other emotions. Share some examples with your partner.

4. Take a few deep breaths and notice if you feel a different sensation in your gut.

> **PLAY TIP:** Younger children may not be familiar with the word "gut." Describing it as their "knowing tummy" can be helpful. With older kids, you can introduce the term "interoception," which is the sense of knowing how you feel based on your body and why this is important.

Empath Vision

SUPPLIES: PEN OR PENCIL

This activity builds upon "Freeze Frame" (page 21) and "Picture Book Feelings Detective" (page 20) but uses made-up scenarios to get your child thinking about different perspectives and how people may feel different things in the same situation. This will help your child with problem-solving and build empathy in peer interactions and conflicts.

1. Read the scenarios on the next page.

2. Think about the different emotions the characters may be feeling.

3. In the space provided, jot down which feelings you think the characters are experiencing and discuss.

Empath Vision Scenarios

Grant and Mila both want to use the basketball. Mila had it first and says she is not going to share.

CHARACTER	FEELING(S)
Grant	
Mila	

Miles wants to stay up late to finish watching the football game, but his dad says he has to go to bed.

CHARACTER	FEELING(S)
Miles	
Dad	

Bruno and Kate are going to get ice cream! Bruno makes his choice quickly—he loves chocolate! Kate is having a hard time deciding which flavor to get and doesn't want to make the wrong choice because it's not every day they go out for ice cream.

CHARACTER	FEELING(S)
Bruno	
Kate	

Maya loves to be included in what her older sister, Olivia, does. Olivia is playing with her blocks and Maya really wants to play, too, and asks to join. Olivia enjoys playing on her own but decides it's okay if Maya plays, too, and says yes.

CHARACTER	FEELING(S)
Maya	
Olivia	

Worry Box

SUPPLIES: PAPER, SCISSORS, PEN OR PENCIL

If your child is like many others, they experience worry from time to time—or maybe most of the time! Identifying our worries makes them more manageable, and this activity is a great way to let your child know it is okay to have worries, but they don't have to allow them to be front and center all the time.

1. Draw a picture of a box. This is your Worry Box. A Worry Box contains or holds our worries so that we don't have to carry our worries alone.

2. Take a moment to think of a few of your worries. Share some of them with the other person.

3. Now it's time to put your worries into the box. You have given them enough of your attention for now, and the box is going to hold those worries for you.

4. To put your worries in your Worry Box, write them in the square.

5. When you are done writing, cut out the square. Fold the square in half and set it aside. This is your way of telling your worries that you are done with them for now.

6. If you need to come back to these worries later, you can always unfold the box for a bit, but don't forget to close it again.

PLAY TIP: **This activity begins to blend in some coping skills along with continued work of identifying feelings. Children who are highly anxious may need additional help containing their worries. Deep breathing and lots of hugs always seem to help when words fail.**

Circle of Calm

SUPPLIES: PAPER, PEN OR PENCIL

Identifying what helps us feel calm is key to being able to reach this state quicker after we have become aroused or escalated. Proactively talking with your child about what helps them feel calm can reduce the intensity of conflicts because you will be able to direct them to these calming activities instead.

1. Think of things that help you feel calm. Share a few of these things with the other person.

2. Now create your Circle of Calm by drawing a small circle in the middle of the paper and then a larger circle around that circle, and so on, until you have a target with about four or five rings around the bull's-eye.

3. Write your name in the bull's-eye.

4. In the next ring, write or draw something that helps you feel calm. Draw or write a few more things that help you feel calm in each of the additional rings of the circle.

5. Share the details of your Circle of Calm with the other person. Discuss how these things help you feel calm.

6. Hang your Circle of Calm somewhere in the house where you can look at it during a conflict so that you can help each other feel calm more quickly next time.

PLAY TIP: Look at your child's Circle of Calm and see if there are small items from it that you can gather in an area of their room, and use this as the guide to making your child's calm down area. (There's more on this in later activities.)

CHAPTER THREE

Communicating Instead of Acting Out

BEING ABLE TO accurately communicate how we are feeling to others decreases confusion or misunderstandings, helps everyone find common ground, and reduces conflict. Children with ODD are often quick to react and struggle with pausing to clearly communicate why they are so upset. This chapter addresses this gap and helps your child appropriately verbalize their thoughts and feelings.

Some of the activities focus on the first part of effective communication: active listening. In these activities, your child will be asked to listen to directives from others and then respond appropriately. This will help habituate your child to following directives and requests from authority. Later in the chapter, your child will learn the importance of tone of voice and positive communication as opposed to acting out when they are frustrated or upset. This will help them learn to communicate productively and reduce inappropriate verbal responses to triggers.

Safe Word

Let's begin this group of activities by learning to communicate some boundaries. This activity will help you and your child create your own boundaries through the use of a safe word, words, or phrase. Safe words communicate that you need time to cool down and you need space away from each other before you react explosively.

1. Take a moment to think about what you would like your safe word(s) or phrase to be. It can be something silly and random or simple and precise.

2. When you are ready, write down your safe word(s) or phrase.

3. Share your safe word(s) or phrase with the other person.

4. Now spend a few moments thinking of scenarios where it would be helpful to use your safe words. Bringing to mind a recent argument here is helpful. Talk about how this argument may have ended differently if one of you had used your safe word(s) or phrase.

5. Discuss together what the plan will be when someone says their safe word(s) or phrase. Be concrete and specific in your plan. What is the first thing you will do when someone says their safe word(s) or phrase? Will you separate from each other? What will you do next?

> PLAY TIP: Some kids may like combining a movement or gesture with their safe word(s) or phrase. Appropriate gestures include signaling stop with your hand or covering part of your face with your hands to visually cut yourself off from the argument.

Body Talk, Part Two

Our bodies are great communicators. The way we are holding our bodies often gives others a very good sense of how we are feeling in that moment. This activity helps your child learn to decipher what someone's body is communicating to the world so that they can respond appropriately.

1. Discuss some of the ways your body communicates how you are feeling to others. Hint: Think about body posture, facial expressions, eye contact, or even how close to or far apart from someone the other person is standing.

2. For each of the following prompts, use your body to communicate the feeling.

    *   *Amy is angry because her mom said she could not go outside unless she puts on a coat.* (How might Amy's body look in this moment?)

    *   *Troy is nervous about playing baseball because he does not think he is any good.* (How might Troy be showing in his body that he is nervous?)

    *   *AJ is feeling left out because when we went outside for recess, all of his friends started playing a game without him.* (What is AJ's body doing to communicate he is feeling left out?)

    *   *Ezra is frustrated because his little brother keeps copying him.* (What are some ways Ezra's body could communicate that he is frustrated?)

3. Continue making up some of your own scenarios or talk about what your bodies are communicating to each other right in this moment.

> **PLAY TIP:** These prompts can get you started, but this activity will work even better if you can use recent examples from your child's life. Change up the names and some of the details to make them more general so your child doesn't feel called out or as if they are getting in trouble.

What Is Active Listening?

SUPPLIES: PEN OR PENCIL

To be able to engage in active listening, your child must have a good understanding of what active listening entails. This activity will help your child describe what active listening means to them and what parts of their body they are engaging when they are using active listening.

1. Think of what it means to use active listening. Here are some helpful prompts:

   - What are your hands doing during active listening?

   - What are your eyes and mouth doing when you are actively listening?

   - How does the rest of your body look? Which way is your body turned? Is it still or moving?

2. In the outline of the body on the next page, write how you use the different body parts when you are engaging in active listening. For example, if you talked about how your hands are gently folded or still when you are actively listening, write on the hands "gently folded" or "still in my lap."

3. Practice using active listening on each other, and have the other person identify which body parts they see you using to actively listen.

> **PLAY TIP:** Make this activity more fun by creating your own cues or signals that the other person is actively listening. Elementary school children will likely know the meaning of "bubble mouth" and how to "turn on their listening ears."

What My Body Does When I'm Actively Listening

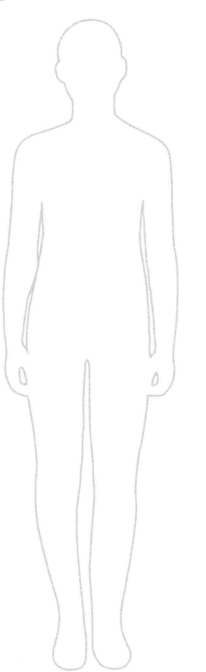

Copy Carly

This is a spin on the classic game Simon Says, but instead of listening for commands, your child will be watching for nonverbal communications or signals. This is a great follow-up activity to "Body Talk, Part Two" (page 41) because it requires your child to look at different parts of the other person's body for signals.

1. Decide who will be Carly first.

2. Carly chooses the movement the other player will make, the nonverbal signal to change, and then the next movement. Here are some examples:

   - Jog in place. When I wink my eye, stand still.

   - Pat your head, and when I touch my nose, rub your belly.

   - Walk in circles around the room. When I wiggle my body, freeze.

   - Jump up and down. When I tug my ear, start clapping your hands.

   - Twist your body. When you see me raise my hand, start laughing.

3. While the other player does the first movement, the other player watches Carly to make the signal for them to start doing the next movement.

4. Continue for a few rounds, and then switch roles.

> **PLAY TIP:** This activity targets multiple skills for your child: active listening, working memory, and sequencing. Don't get discouraged if it takes a few rounds for your child to get the hang of it. You are working on growing skills!

Find My Phone

SUPPLIES: AN ELECTRONIC DEVICE

This is a fun activity to do when your child won't stop asking to play with your phone or tablet! Turn it into a game of hide-and-seek in which your child has to listen to cues from you to figure out where the item is hidden. This game not only targets communication and listening skills but also helps create more playfulness in your parent–child relationship.

1. Decide who will be the "hider" and who will be the "seeker" first.

2. The seeker closes their eyes while the hider hides the device somewhere in the room. (Alternatively, the seeker leaves the room to increase the difficulty.) When the device is hidden, the hider says, "Ready!"

3. The seeker begins looking for the device based on the hider's hot and cold clues. Hider says, "Hot" when the seeker is close to the item and "Cold" when they are moving farther away from it. Continue until the seeker finds the item, and then switch roles.

PLAY TIP: Get as silly and as animated as you can with your hot and cold clues! Clues such as "Burning hot!", "On fire!", and "Brrr, getting colder!" can make the activity more fun for younger children. For older children, challenge them by giving the temperatures in degrees.

Banana Ball Toss

SUPPLIES: BALL OR SOFT ITEM SUCH AS A STUFFED ANIMAL OR SMALL PILLOW

This activity taps into the skill of differentiation—the ability to filter out words and zero in on what's important. This helps your child with focusing on directions and limits set by you. You and your child will be bonding and playing a fun physical game while helping your child develop active listening.

1. Decide who will be player one. This person gets the ball first.

2. Player two begins saying many different and silly words, but player one is listening only for the word "banana."

3. When player two says "banana," player one tosses the ball to player two, and then the roles reverse.

4. Keep the game going for several rounds.

> PLAY TIP: You can increase the challenge of this activity by adding in some commands such as "Throw it" and "Drop it" or using a lot of words that start with B, like "bicycle." This helps with communication by challenging your child to listen, filter out unnecessary words the other person is saying, and inhibit a response.

At the Zoo

This game continues the development of active listening as a key part of effective communication. It gets your child used to listening to and following commands and cues within the setting of a playful game while developing critically important skills for when you are setting limits and correcting their behavior.

1. Think of animals you would see at the zoo. Discuss some of your favorite zoo animals.

2. Decide who will be the "zookeeper" and who will be the "zoo animals" first.

3. The zookeeper says, "Today at the zoo, I see a (*fill in the blank*)." Some ideas include tiger, gorilla, zebra, and snake.

4. After hearing the name of the animal, the other player makes sounds and movements that animal would make.

5. The zookeeper says the phrase again with a different animal, and play continues.

6. Switch roles after a couple of rounds.

> **PLAY TIP:** Parents who are willing to really get into character are sure to get a big laugh out of their kids! If your child has never been to a zoo, find a book about zoo animals or spend time on the internet looking up some of your favorite zoo animals to show them.

Sweet and Sour

SUPPLIES: PEN OR PENCIL

In this activity, you will be communicating with your child in a nonthreatening way about each of your likes and dislikes as well as high moments and challenges. Talking to your child about their preferences builds the communication between you in general but also increases your child's window of tolerance for talking about more vulnerable topics.

1. Look at the worksheet on the next page. Notice the columns labeled "sweet" and "sour."

2. Things you like or enjoy will go in the "sweet" column, and things you do not like will go in the "sour" column. (The second person can do this on a separate sheet of paper.)

3. Discuss some of your sweets, or favorite things—for example, favorite foods, movies, songs, and superhero characters.

4. Discuss some of your sour items, or things you really do not enjoy. Think of the chores you hate the most or activities that are challenging or hard that you do not like to do.

5. Now, for each category in the worksheet, write your sweet (likes) and sour (dislikes) answers.

6. When you're done, compare your answers and talk about any similarities or differences.

> PLAY TIP: This activity can help you and your child bond and feel more connected through open communication about positive moments you both enjoy and gets the dialogue going for things your child does not like to do and communicating these preferences in a calm moment.

My Sweet and Sours

CATEGORY	SWEET	SOUR
FAMILY DINNERS In the "sweet" column, write what you like about family dinners. In the "sour" column, write what you currently don't like about family dinners.		
SCHOOL In the "sweet" column, write your favorite parts about school. In the "sour" column, write your least favorite parts about school.		
ACTIVITIES In the "sweet" column, write some of your favorite activities (for example, sports, after-school activities, hobbies). In the "sour" column, write a few things you have to do but do not enjoy doing.		
MY DAY In the "sweet" column, write about parts of your day that you really enjoy. In the "sour" column, write about the difficult or challenging parts of your day.		
MY FAMILY In the "sweet" column, write things you like about your family. In the "sour" column, write some things you would like to see change within your family.		

Balloon Lava

SUPPLIES: UNINFLATED BALLOON

This game is one of the favorites in the playroom at my office! It requires clear and quick communication as well as fast thinking and active listening from the other person. It also involves a little physical movement, which is great for venting any pent-up frustrations your child may be carrying.

1. Practice deep breathing by taking several deep breaths and blowing up the balloon. Tie it off or get help when it's the size you want.

2. Hit the balloon back and forth in the air without letting it touch the floor to get some practice.

3. Now decide who will be the "referee" and who will be the "player" first.

4. The player hits the ball in the air without letting it touch the floor.

5. The referee then calls out a body part, and the player is only allowed to use that body part to keep the balloon in the air. For example, if the referee calls out, "Pinky finger!", the player is only allowed to use their pinky finger to keep the balloon in the air. The referee calls out a new body part every five to ten seconds.

6. Switch roles after several different body parts have been called out.

> **PLAY TIP:** Be creative with the body parts—think elbows, knees, and nose! To challenge older children, fill the balloon with less air (so it falls more quickly to the ground) and be more specific with body parts such as the *left* elbow or *right* knee.

Things Toss

SUPPLIES: BALL OR SOFT ITEM

Adapted from The Game of THINGS, a popular party game, this activity is intended to increase positive communication between you and your child and also create a moment of bonding and closeness. You will learn more about your child through this open communication, and your child will feel empowered and heard in your parent–child relationship.

1. The goal of this game is to think of as many things as you can in a particular category. Examples of categories include types of cars, flavors of ice cream, fruits and vegetables, cities and places, and words that begin with a specific letter such as L.

2. Decide who will choose the first category and give that person the ball.

3. Stand across from each other at a reasonable distance for your child's age and ability.

4. The first player names one thing in that category and then passes the ball to the other player, who then names one thing in that category before passing the ball back.

5. When one player cannot think of any more things in that category, the round ends.

6. The next round begins with the other player choosing the next category and naming something in that category. Continue for a few rounds so each person gets to choose the category a few times.

> PLAY TIP: This game is great at getting your child to open up and start communicating because they are distracted by the tossing of the ball. For older kids, you can tap into this by giving categories such as "a time you felt hurt" or "friends you enjoy the most right now."

Complimentary Crusaders

SUPPLIES: PAPER, PEN OR PENCIL

You have been working diligently on the communication skill of listening. Let's now shift to the other important skill: respectful and positive *expressive* communication. This activity specifically helps your child learn how to communicate the strengths they see in the other person. Learning to focus on strengths will help your child reduce defiance and conflict by finding the positives.

1. Discuss the meaning of the word "compliment" and talk about a time when you each received a compliment from another person. What was the compliment? Who gave it to you? How did it feel to receive the compliment?

2. Now it's time to give some compliments to each other! This is your opportunity to let the other person know all the kind things you think and feel toward them but maybe don't always communicate. Think of five compliments you can give to the other person and write them down.

3. When you are both done writing, read the compliments out loud to each other.

4. Talk about your experience of hearing the other person give you these compliments.

5. Now talk about how you felt after giving compliments to the other person. How was this different from receiving the compliments? Which felt better—giving or receiving? How can you find ways to give *genuine* compliments to the other person throughout the day?

PLAY TIP: Some days are tough, and you might not be in the mood to give compliments, but these are the exact moments when stopping to think of one positive compliment you can give can make all the difference in the world. Even if your child is yelling or screaming, if they kept safe hands and did not become aggressive, give the compliment and verbalize this success later when they are calm.

Friendly Feather Tickles

SUPPLIES: A FEATHER OR ANY SOFT ITEM

This activity will help you and your child practice clearly letting each other know your boundaries and where you feel comfortable being touched or tickled with a feather. This requires the skills of both active listening and clear communication. Working on communication with your child will help ensure that they are learning the skills to accurately articulate what their goals or intentions are, which will help keep frustrations lower and emotions calmer when disagreements arise.

1. Decide who will be the "commander" and who will be the "tickler" first.

2. The commander gives a clear command of where on the body they want to be tickled by the feather. For example, "Tickle me on the back of my hand" or "Tickle me on my forehead."

3. The tickler listens to the commands and then tickles just that part of the other person's body. The tickler must listen closely to the commands, and only the part of the body that the commander states can be tickled.

4. The round ends and roles are switched if the tickler touches a part of the body that has not been specified or after a few body parts have been named.

5. Continue the game until each person gets a few rounds being the commander or the tickler.

> PLAY TIP: Make your commands challenging for older ticklers, such as only tickling the big toe or thumbnail. Children who are sensitive to sensory input may not like the feel of a feather; different materials can be used, or you can just tap the named areas with your fingertips.

Feel/When Statements

SUPPLIES: PEN OR PENCIL

Many children blame others for how they are feeling. Negative emotions can be hard to own and even more difficult to communicate to others. This activity helps your child reframe their communication by beginning their sentences with "I feel . . ." as opposed to "You made me feel . . ." This helps communication remain effective and focused on collaboration rather than on blame.

1. Discuss how beginning your feeling statements with the phrase "I feel" helps you take ownership of your own emotions.

2. Read the prompts on the next page and fill in the rest of the sentence for each. (The other person can use a separate piece of paper.)

3. When you have finished all the statements, share what you wrote with the other person.

4. To keep the conversation going, use these discussion questions:

   • As the listener, how did it feel to hear the other person communicate about how they were feeling?

   • How is this different from hearing someone say you made them feel a certain way?

   • Which way is more likely to create conflict?

   • Which way is more likely to communicate a desire to resolve the problem or work through things?

   • Give examples of how you can use more "I feel" statements throughout your day.

> **PLAY TIP:** Modeling is key! The more you can model a behavior, the more likely your child will begin to incorporate that behavior into their life—for better or worse! The more you are able to model your own "I feel . . ." statements throughout the week, the more you will notice your child communicating ownership of their emotions and taking more responsibility.

I feel angry when ....

....

....

....

I feel excited when ....

....

....

....

I feel sad when ....

....

....

....

I feel loved when ....

....

....

....

I feel hurt when ....

....

....

....

I feel proud when ....

....

....

....

Superhero Vision

SUPPLIES: SUNGLASSES (OPTIONAL)

Some superheroes are able to see through walls. With good, clear communication, you can be a superhero with X-ray vision, too. This game is similar to 20 Questions, but instead of one player asking questions, the other player will be giving descriptive statements.

1. Decide who will be the "superhero" first. That player puts on the sunglasses, if using, or imaginary X-ray vision glasses.

2. The other player looks around the room and chooses a secret item with just their eyes. They do not touch or play with it; they choose it, look away, and keep the image in their mind.

3. The other player now describes the secret item to the superhero as well as they can without naming it. For example, if you chose the light switch, you might say, "It is white and square and is located on the wall next to the door."

4. The superhero uses their X-ray vision to "see" the item in the other person's mind and guesses what it is.

5. If they guess incorrectly, the other player provides more details until the superhero guesses what the item is.

6. Switch roles and continue play.

> **PLAY TIP:** Older kids may feel too cool to pretend to be a superhero or use props, so this game can be altered for a more grown-up feel by simply rotating who gets to be "It"—as in "You're it!"—or who gets to describe the secret item to the second player.

Tone of Voice

This activity really brings your and your child's attention to the importance and significance of tone of voice when communicating with others. Recognizing how tone affects the outcome of a conversation is a key skill for children with ODD to develop. This game targets this skill in a fun and nonthreatening way.

1. Discuss how there are different tones of voice and ways of saying things, and then get ready to showcase all your different voices and animated expressions!

2. Read each of these statements three times, following the instructions in steps 3 to 5:

   - I'm working on it.

   - I'm doing the best I can.

   - I need more time.

3. The first time you read the statement, say it in a calm or happy voice.

4. The second time you read the statement, say it in an irritated or frustrated voice.

5. The third time you read the statement, say it in a mad voice.

6. After each player has a turn, discuss how different the same statement sounded when you said it different ways. What is the difference between the frustrated and mad voices? (Hint: Think of the level of intensity.) Which voice was the nicest or most pleasant to hear when the other person said it? How did you feel as the other person was saying the statement different ways?

> **PLAY TIP:** Most children I've worked with also enjoy saying these statements in a sarcastic tone of voice. If you model a sarcastic tone for your child, you can start a conversation about how it feels to hear someone using sarcasm with you and how people might respond.

The Way You Say

This activity takes "Tone of Voice" a step further by focusing on the importance of a kind and respectful tone and how your child can harness the power of respectful communication to help get their needs met.

1. Put yourself in the following scenarios as you move through each step and focus on *the way* you make each statement. Take turns with your partner so that you each have a chance to make the statement.

    - You are frustrated with homework and need some help. Ask for help in a calm, respectful tone.

    - You want to stay up late to finish the last quarter of a sports game. Practice asking your partner nicely if you can watch a bit more.

    - Your friend asked you to join a game of tag, but you really don't feel like playing. Make a kind statement that lets your friend know you are passing on the game without hurting their feelings.

    - Someone calls you an inappropriate name. Respond in a way that lets them know you do not like the name but that won't get you in trouble, too.

    - Your friend accidentally cuts in front of you in line. Communicate to the friend in a respectful way what the expectation is for lining up.

    > PLAY TIP: You can make this more personal by adding in scenarios from your child's recent social experiences. Talk about how to politely turn down an invitation to play or how to let friends know you are feeling left out without reacting in anger.

Positive Alternatives

It's time to work on cognitive reframing and cognitive challenging (both skills practiced in cognitive behavioral therapy, or CBT) to inhibit aggressive verbal communication and choose positive communication instead. Your child will practice replacing negative outbursts and statements with respectful and kind communication to help make better choices and reduce conflict.

1. Discuss how finding positive alternatives to angry yelling can help keep everyone calm and keep them out of trouble.

2. Take turns with your partner, reading each prompt out loud and completing the statement. Talk through your response with your partner.

   - Instead of screaming, I will communicate that I am angry by . . .

   - Instead of throwing an item when I am frustrated, I will communicate my frustration by . . .

   - When I am feeling hurt, I will communicate this by . . .

   - When I am feeling lonely, I will communicate this by saying . . .

   - Instead of slamming the door when I am mad, I will communicate my mad feelings by . . .

   - I will stop myself from hurting others and instead communicate my big, uncomfortable feelings by . . .

3. Discuss how reframing each of these responses to something positive will help reduce conflict and consequences.

4. Now act out a few of the scenarios to practice the positive alternatives.

> **PLAY TIP:** Think back to the "Feel/When Statements" activity on page 54 and help your child with responses that begin with "I feel" when completing the statements. This will help them take ownership and responsibility for their feelings and communicate them in a productive way.

When I Say

SUPPLIES: PEN OR PENCIL

This activity is essentially a continuation of "Positive Alternatives" but helps clarify communication by helping your child more accurately communicate how they are feeling or what they are needing. This helps you better understand how to respond and give your child what they need, thereby increasing your parent–child connection and attunement.

1. Discuss how sometimes we say one thing but feel something totally different! Talk about why this might happen (for example, we are embarrassed by our feelings, we don't think the other person would understand, or we are confused and don't even know what we are feeling!).

2. Read each statement on the next page and have your child write their responses in the space provided.

3. When they are finished, discuss their answers. Remember that there is no right or wrong way to feel. Let your child guide their responses and be open to their communication of how they are feeling. You are focusing on more open communication and allowing your child to take ownership of how they want to express themselves in a productive way.

> PLAY TIP: This activity is meant to be a bit challenging and require your child to really think about their inner feelings and how they are communicating those. Give them time to come up with their responses and try not to jump in too quickly with your own answers.

When I Say . . .

Sometimes when I say, "I am fine," it really means ....

....

....

Sometimes when I say, "I am bored," I am really feeling ....

....

....

Sometimes when I yell, "Leave me alone!", what I really need is ....

....

....

Sometimes when I say, "I don't care," I really feel ....

....

....

Sometimes when I ask for help with things I can do on my own, I am
really saying, " ....

....

.... " .

Sometimes when I say, "I can't do it," I am really feeling ....

....

....

Peace Circle

SUPPLIES: A SMALL TOY OR TALKING STICK

A Peace Circle offers children a safe and calm way to talk about conflict. When we try to solve problems in the moment, we are often met with resistance and opposition. When you use a designated Peace Circle to talk through solutions to conflict, you can tap into your child's inner wisdom and problem-solving skills. During this activity, the item is held by the person whose turn it is to speak.

1. Sit across from your child. This is your Peace Circle. Hold up the item and explain that only the person holding it can speak ("they have the floor"). This gives each person time to communicate without being interrupted or corrected.

2. Ask your child to think of a recent conflict. This can be a conflict with a friend, you, a sibling, or anyone else. Let your child know you will be thinking of a recent conflict, too.

3. As you hand the item to your child, ask them to talk about that conflict, practice communicating how they felt in the moment of the conflict, and try to identify what they needed in that moment. (Common needs include needing to be heard, needing to be understood, needing space, needing freedom, needing to be included or loved, and needing independence.)

4. If you are not holding the item, your job is to just listen.

5. When your child passes the item back to you, it's your turn to talk about a recent conflict and communicate what you were feeling and needing in the moment.

6. Take a few turns doing this.

> PLAY TIP: This activity can be used anytime during the day. Catch the conflict before it escalates by retrieving the talking item and handing it to your child. With practice, they will learn to communicate their feelings and needs to help increase positive communication instead of reacting negatively.

Snaps for Me!

SUPPLIES: PAPER; PEN, COLORED PENCILS, MARKERS, OR CRAYONS

In this activity, your child is encouraged to think of positive statements that best describe some of their strengths. Sometimes our days feel so busy and full that we neglect to stop and ponder our positive aspects and articulate the things we do well. This activity helps make this behavior more common so your child catches themselves doing things right more often.

1. Snapping is quieter and calmer than loud claps and cheers. Discuss that for this activity, a "snap" is a compliment, an encouraging statement, or a way to offer recognition for a job well done.

2. Think and talk about some of your strengths, encouraging your child to come up with their own. Often we can easily find encouraging words for others, but this can be difficult to do for ourselves. If this is difficult at first, encourage your child to practice looking for the positives about themselves.

3. On the top of the paper, have your child write "Snaps for Me!" and list or draw their strengths below it.

4. Discuss the positive statements and strengths your child wrote down.

5. Your child can color or doodle on the "Snaps for Me!" page while you continue talking about the importance of giving ourselves snaps by communicating positive and encouraging statements to ourselves.

PLAY TIP: Some children really struggle with positive attention or praise. This activity helps increase the tolerance for this as they are working to praise themselves as opposed to receiving external praise (which can increase pressure to perform and result in anxiety). Try to keep your reactions smaller (think of snapping versus clapping), allowing your child to quietly acknowledge their strengths.

CHAPTER FOUR

Practicing Self-Control and Returning to Calm

SELF-REGULATING THEIR BEHAVIOR and emotions to return to calm is a skill that children do not naturally develop on their own. It must be modeled, practiced, and reinforced for it to become a go-to habit. The activities in this chapter focus on developing and strengthening the skills of self-regulation (control of one's body and reactions) so that defiant and oppositional behaviors are reduced.

These activities cover skills related to self-calming, such as deep breathing, mindful movements, and physical release of tension to decrease the intensity of emotions so they can be better managed. They also touch on self-evaluation (the ability to check in with ourselves to assess how we are doing and readjust our behavior) to help your child learn to recognize when they need to self-direct to calming activities or step away to engage in calming movements or deep breathing.

Stoplight Signals

SUPPLIES: PEN OR PENCIL; RED, YELLOW, AND GREEN CRAYONS OR COLORED PENCILS

Let's start with a little self-evaluation activity to help you assess how well your child is able to pause and evaluate their feelings in the moment. This activity is simply focused on increasing awareness—not on the techniques or interventions *yet*. Your child must first have a solid understanding of what each stage (red, yellow, and green) feels like in their body to begin working on self-regulation.

1. Look at the picture of the stoplight on the next page. The stoplight is made up of three sections. Label the top section "red," the middle section "yellow," and the bottom section "green."

2. Discuss with your child the green section at the bottom of the stoplight. This is the starting phase of calmness and control and when they have access to the part of their brain that controls their thinking. How do they know they are in the green? What does green feel like in their body when they are calm?

3. Now discuss the yellow section. This is when they notice they are beginning to get mad, but they are not quite red yet—it is more of a warning that they need to calm themselves down. Try to think of a few examples of this stage with your child and ask them to think about how this feels in their body.

4. Then discuss with your child the triggers or events that make them feel angry. This is the top part of the stoplight. In the red stage, they no longer have access to the "green" section and are functioning in the more primitive part of the brain. Describe how feelings of anger grow and how when we are angry, the light changes from yellow to red. Ask, "What does red feel like in your body, and how do you know you are 'seeing red'? What are some clues that you are moving from yellow to red? What does it feel like to lose control of your body sometimes?"

5. While discussing the stages, your child can use the crayons or markers to color in the sections of the traffic light.

> **PLAY TIP:** Visual cues work great for some children. If your child loves visual cues, have them write their responses or cues for each color on the image and hang it in their bedroom. You can point to it when you see them leaving the green stage and ask your child stop and assess which stage they are going into. This awareness can help them stop from reaching "red."

Bubble Breaths

SUPPLIES: A BOTTLE OF BUBBLES AND TWO WANDS

These next few activities focus on breathing techniques to help your child learn the skills of self-regulation and how to self-calm. This activity is a fun and playful way to help your child work on deep breathing while simultaneously connecting with you.

1. Discuss the skills required to blow bubbles. Do you blow fast or slow? How do you make big bubbles? How do you make lots of little bubbles?

2. Give each partner a bubble wand. First practice taking big, slow breaths to make a bubble as big as you can. See who can make the biggest bubble.

3. Next, try to make lots of smaller bubbles. See who can make the most little bubbles.

4. Discuss the difference between the two types of bubbles. What did you notice that was different about your breathing? Which style of breathing helped you feel more calm or more in control? Did either style of breathing cause you to feel tightness in your chest?

5. Continue blowing bubbles together and practice making more of the bigger bubbles together with longer, deeper breaths.

> PLAY TIP: This activity can be done in the moment with or without bubbles! Once your child has practiced the muscle memory needed to make big bubbles, they can pantomime this anytime to slow their heart rate and help them return to a calm state.

4-6-8 Breathing

This activity targets deep breathing a little bit more directly than the previous activity. Controlled breathing, such as in this exercise, is the fastest way to de-escalate emotions and help our bodies return to calm. Even taking three deep breaths can change one's brain chemistry and reduce stress hormones.

1. Warm up your lungs by taking a few deep breaths together.

2. Now slowly inhale for four seconds, filling your lungs completely with air.

3. Once your lungs are full, hold your breath for six seconds.

4. Slowly begin to let the air out through your mouth; try to take eight seconds to complete your exhale. If all the air leaves your lungs before the eight seconds are over, try again and see how long you can make it the next time.

5. Repeat steps 2 through 4 a few more times.

6. This time, breathe in for four seconds, hold for six seconds, and then exhale for eight seconds through just your nose.

7. Try this a few times and discuss whether you notice a difference between mouth and nose breathing.

> **PLAY TIP:** For more advanced deep breathers, try the reverse: Inhale for eight seconds, hold for six seconds, and release for four seconds. Children often find it a little easier to do the longer exhale than the longer inhale.

Putty Smash

SUPPLIES: PLAY-DOH, MALLEABLE DOUGH, OR MODELING CLAY

Now that you have some practice with deep breathing, it's time to work on physical ways to release tension and stress. Finding a physical outlet for emotions helps regulate our bodies so that we can regain control. This and the next few activities focus on the proprioceptive input of pushing against things or mashing things to help calm our bodies.

1. Spend the first few minutes just playing with the dough and warming it up in your hands, noticing any sensations that come into your awareness. (Is the clay cold? Does it warm up as you use it? Is part of it dried out?)

2. Roll the dough around in your hands as many times as needed to make a ball, seeing if you can smooth out all the cracks.

3. Next, use a flat hand to firmly press the ball, smashing it into the playing surface. Keep squishing and pressing the dough with your hand until it is completely flat.

4. Make a few more dough balls and continue practicing squishing or flattening them.

> PLAY TIP: This exercise is simple yet effective! It helps by both working as a distraction when your child needs help calming down and keeping their hands busy without hitting. It also provides firm input when their hands press against the dough, which helps regulate the brain.

Hulk Press

This activity continues the proprioceptive input from "Putty Smash" but is done using their hands and yours with no other supplies necessary. This way, you can have your child to do it anytime and anywhere you notice that they are becoming escalated. It provides a physical means to release anger through pressing palms together, inhibiting your child from making a fist.

1. Discuss the characteristics of the Hulk from Marvel Comics. If you don't know much about this superhero, do a quick internet search.

2. Stand up and hold out your palms, facing the other person, as if you are going to give each other a high five with both hands.

3. Bring your palms together like a high five but keep your hands touching and pressing together.

4. Now ask your child to imagine that they are the Hulk. While your hands are pressed together, have your child firmly push with their Hulk strength against your hands. Try to keep your own hands firm and use your own Hulk strength to push back to create resistance.

5. The goal is to have both people pushing into the hands so that your hands do not move but you are holding still and pushing against each other.

6. Do a few sets of Hulk presses for five seconds each and take a break between each round.

> PLAY TIP: The biggest key here is the energy and force being released through the physical tension of pushing your palms together. This exercise is useful when your child needs a distraction because they are becoming agitated and need a quick outlet for their hands to remain safe.

Pillow Hugs

SUPPLIES: PILLOW OR STUFFED ANIMAL

This activity helps your child with another outlet for emotions to achieve calmness. If you continue to provide outlets and different options to release pent-up emotions and anger, your child is sure to discover what works best for them and, with enough practice, will be able to self-direct to these activities.

1. Think about and discuss a recent time when you felt angry.

2. Next, squeeze the pillow as hard as you can with all your might for ten seconds while the other person counts out loud.

3. Relax for a few seconds, and repeat two to three times. Your arms should feel tired and worn out.

4. Now think about the same situation you identified earlier that made you feel angry. Do you feel any differently now that you squeezed the pillow a few times? If not, squeeze it a few more times until it no longer makes you mad when you think about the situation.

> **PLAY TIP:** This is an activity you can guide your child to in the midst of becoming escalated, with kind words such as "I notice you are starting to become frustrated and wonder if now would be a good time to go do a few pillow hugs."

Dinosaur Stomps

This activity is the last of the exercises focusing on a physical release of tension to calm the body, and this one focuses on releasing tension through the feet as opposed to through the hands. This one is good for a more active child who needs a little more physical movement to get a proper release.

1. Take a few moments to imagine yourself as a dinosaur. Which dinosaur are you? Do you have horns or spikes? Do you crawl on all fours or walk on two feet?

2. Have fun doing some dinosaur moves around the room to warm up your body.

3. Now imagine there is a puddle of water in front of you and the dinosaur wants to make a big HUGE dinosaur splash in the puddle! Stomp and press your foot into the puddle a few times to make a big splash!

4. After you have made big splashes, imagine that the dinosaur needs to stomp through the mud to make big footsteps. Take a few big stomps around the room, pressing down through your dinosaur foot to make a footprint in the pretend mud.

5. Talk with your partner about how you feel after making these big stomps. Do you feel more relaxed? Are your legs a bit tired? Dinosaurs sure have to work hard to make such big splashes and footprints!

> PLAY TIP: This exercise is good for younger kids as it requires a little fun and imagination. For older children, instead of dinosaur stomps, just have them visualize pushing all their feelings out through the bottom of their feet and into the ground as firmly as they can, taking a few steps to do this two to three times on each foot.

I Can

SUPPLIES: PEN OR PENCIL

This activity helps bring the awareness back to internal methods of control and teaches your child to focus on what they can control and let go of the rest. Learning to focus on only our own reactions to situations instead of what the other person is doing is a big lesson for any child, but especially for those with ODD.

1. Look at the worksheet for this activity on the next page and prepare to write in your responses. The other person can use a separate sheet of paper.

2. Begin by describing a recent event, experience, or conflict.

3. Now complete the categories of things you *can* control in that type of situation. For answers here, think about your body and your emotions. (Hint: We can't control other people's emotions, but we *can* control our own.) Also, think back to some of the breathing exercises you have tried and ways they helped you learn to control your body.

4. After you have written a few responses, discuss what you wrote with your partner. Was it easy or difficult to identify things you can control?

5. Next, complete the categories of things that are out of your control. (Hint: You can't control what some else said or did or might choose to say or do.)

6. After you have written a few responses, discuss what you wrote with your partner. Discuss how it is sometimes really difficult to let go of these things that are out of our control. Identify which are the hardest to let go of.

> PLAY TIP: Developing some affirmations to go along with this activity can be helpful for some kids. Phrases such as "You take care of you" or "I am in control of my body" are some helpful ones. See what resonates with your child.

Things I Can and Cannot Control

Describe the situation (event, experience, or conflict): ....

....

....

....

....

WHAT I *CAN* CONTROL . . .	WHAT I *CANNOT* CONTROL . . .

Waterfall Counting

This activity is one of the most common ones I have children in my office practice. It can be done anytime, anywhere, and it brings the focus back internally by using mindfulness to block out all thoughts other than the counting. I have seen this de-escalate situations many times and help return the child to a calm state of mind.

1. Warm up by taking a few deep breaths.

2. Take a moment to identify a recent stressful situation. It can be anything related to school, homework, friends, or family.

3. Once you have it in mind, discuss the situation with your partner. You may notice your chest getting tighter or your heart rate increasing just because you are thinking about this! That's okay. The next part of the activity will help.

4. Now that you have increased the stress a tiny bit by thinking about this stressful situation, practice bringing your heart rate back down and calming your body. Begin by counting from one all the way to ten. When you get to ten, pause for a second, then start at ten, and count back down to one.

5. Continue this "waterfall" pattern (from one to ten and back down ten to one) five to six times or until you feel your body relax and the stressful thoughts leave your mind.

> **PLAY TIP:** Because this can be done silently in the child's head, it's a great one to teach your child to use at school when they become escalated or stressed; no one will know they are doing it.

Mindful Meditation

Mindfulness allows us to filter out unnecessary and distracting thoughts and focus solely on the present moment. This helps calm the body and is great practice.

1. A meditative activity is one that can be completed without thinking too much about what you are doing and is often repetitive, such as brushing your teeth or washing the dishes. Discuss meditation, mindfulness, and what it means to be connected to and aware of our bodies and thoughts.

2. Read the following script slowly to your child:

    a. Find a comfortable seated position. Pay special attention to the here-and-now sensations in your body as I speak.

    b. Gently close your eyes. Take three slow, deep breaths.

    c. Begin to scan your body, starting at your feet. Are you wearing shoes or socks? Do your feet feel cold or warm?

    d. Move up your body, noticing all the sensations in your legs and middle section.

    e. Notice the sensation of your bottom pressing against the floor or your chair.

    f. Move up your back and chest. Is your chest tight or airy?

    g. Continue scanning your fingertips and up through your arms.

    h. Now notice your neck and shoulders, paying special attention to any tightness.

    i. Finally, scan your head and face. Relax all your facial muscles, releasing your jaw, relaxing your mouth, and allowing it to open if needed.

    j. Imagine stretching up through the top of your head as if a light were beaming out through the highest point in your body.

    k. When you are done scanning, take a few more slow, deep breaths.

> **PLAY TIP:** Once your child has the general idea of this mindful meditation practice, you can have them do this body scan anytime they begin to become escalated and need a moment to distract from the environment and focus on internal sensations.

Cookie Challenge

SUPPLIES: TWO SMALL COOKIES OR TREATS, TIMER, CHOICE OF DISTRACTIONS

This activity takes the mindfulness practice a step further. For this activity, your child is required to use distraction techniques, restraint, and positive self-talk.

1. Place a few activities your child likes to do on the table beforehand to serve as potential distractions (paper and crayons, LEGOs, stickers).

2. With your child seated at the table and without making any mention of the activities, set one cookie on the table and say, "I am going to leave the room for five minutes. I will return when the five-minute timer goes off. If this cookie is still here when I return, you will get to eat a second cookie, too. If you eat this first cookie by the time I return, you will not get a second one."

3. Set the timer and leave the room for five minutes. It is up to your child to decide how they spend the time (as long as they are being safe and not in danger).

4. Return when the timer goes off. If the first cookie is still there, give your child both cookies. If not, put the second cookie back in the box and try again another time.

PLAY TIP: **Children who have the most success with this challenge often use distraction techniques. This will help your child learn to distract their mind when they are getting upset or angry and need to think about something else so that they do not lash out in anger.**

Mirror, Mirror

This activity involves one person copying, or mirroring, the other person's movements and expressions. This skill requires mindfulness and concentration, both of which distract from triggering situations and can help your child return to calm after a difficult or challenging task. This is a great one to try right after a stressful homework session!

1. Sit cross-legged in front of each other, and discuss how a mirror reflects the image in front of it and what this means to each of you.

2. Your child will be looking in the mirror first, and you will be the mirror, reflecting their movements to illustrate how this is done. Remember, a mirror does not judge or confront; it simply mirrors, or copies, exactly what it sees. As the mirror, you will copy your partner's movements, only doing what they do; do not add any of your own movements.

3. After a minute or two, switch roles.

> **PLAY TIP:** When you model this activity by being the mirror first, your child can better understand the task and what is expected. Add in a challenge by making smaller movements that require your child to really focus on you when they are mirroring you.

Fortune Teller

SUPPLIES: A BALL OR OTHER ROUND ITEM (OPTIONAL)

This activity places your child in the position of the all-knowing fortune teller, and you get to be the one seeking advice for the future. You will present different scenarios, and your child will predict possible outcomes or consequences for behavior and give you advice on how to respond.

1. Place the round item, if using, on a table between you and your child to make believe it is a fortune teller's crystal ball.

2. Present each of the following scenarios to your child one at a time, and as they wave their hands over the "crystal ball," have them predict what will happen in the future as a consequence of your actions.

   - I accidentally broke my friend's LEGO creation and hid the broken pieces in their closet.

   - My sister grabbed the toy I was using. I got so angry that I yelled and pushed her down.

   - My parents asked if I had any homework, and I didn't feel like doing it, so I said no.

   - My friend and I were having a disagreement. I started to get mad, so I walked away, went to my room, and shut the door.

3. Keep in mind that some of the situations may have a few different possible outcomes. It's okay for the fortune teller to make a few predictions for each scenario. Also, they may see only possible positive outcomes, only negative consequences, or a mix of the two.

> **PLAY TIP:** You can add in personalized scenarios that typically occur in your home. Does your child regularly struggle with putting things away? Make up a scenario and have your child look into the future to see what might happen if an item is lost.

Reach for the Stars

This and the next few activities focus on techniques to regain self-control by teaching your child to control their physical body while incorporating some mindfulness techniques into the movements. This activity in particular is a great one to use to help regulate your child's mind and body through slow, controlled movements. Be sure to choose an area of your home where your child can freely move their arms about and twist their body without bumping into anything.

1. Get ready to relax and stretch your body!

2. Take a few deep breaths to center yourself.

3. Imagine that your arms and legs are beginning to grow. They are stretching and growing so long that you can almost reach the sky!

4. Now stretch your arms up as high as you can into the sky, reaching as tall as you can. You might come up on your tiptoes to reach even higher. Imagine your arms being pulled and extended to reach even a few more inches.

5. Lower your feet back to the ground and relax your arms by your side.

6. Repeat the stretch a few more times, slowly raising your arms each time and reaching for the stars as high as you can.

> PLAY TIP: This is a great preventive technique to increase self-control. Incorporate this mindful stretch into homework time, right before family dinners, or anytime you need your child to be more centered and display a greater amount of self-control.

Job Well Done

SUPPLIES: PEN OR PENCIL

This activity helps your child with self-control by asking them to think about a recent conflict and evaluate their choice of actions. By asking your child to first focus on what they did right, this activity helps strengthen their self-control skills while also pointing out areas for improvement.

1. Ask your child to think about a recent conflict within the past week. This conflict can be one they had with parents, a friend, a sibling, or anyone else. If they have trouble identifying a conflict, offer prompts for them to think about something that made them feel mad or a situation that was really challenging or difficult.

2. Once the situation is identified, talk through together what they did well and what choices may have gotten them in trouble. Be sure to identify what they did well first, even if it was something minor. Successes include yelling but keeping safe hands or removing themselves to their room to calm down even if they slammed the door. (Slamming doors would then be identified as the area to improve, but success would be walking away from the upsetting situation.)

3. After you have talked through the situation together, have your child complete the worksheet on the next page.

4. Discuss how you can help your child focus on the areas for improvement next time and whether you can develop code words or signals that will help them remember to work on this skill in the moment.

> PLAY TIP: This activity brings to light the importance of focusing on positives and praising your child for even small moments of self-control. With continued practice, those moments will become more frequent, but you first have to offer your child acknowledgment and praise.

Briefly describe the recent conflict:

_____

_____

_____

_____

_____

_____

WHAT I DID WELL IN THIS SITUATION:	WHAT I WILL WORK ON FOR NEXT TIME:

Noodle Dance

SUPPLIES: FAVORITE SONG OR MUSIC (OPTIONAL)

This activity introduces a progressive muscle relaxation skill to increase your child's self-control and calmness in their body. Your child will practice tensing and releasing their muscles to promote a sense of relaxation and de-escalating emotions when things get heated during an argument.

1. Play your favorite song or, if you prefer peace and quiet, that's fine, too.

2. Get ready to tighten and squeeze each of your muscle groups for five seconds. After the five-second squeeze, relax that muscle group. Follow this series:

   - Face and jaw
   - Neck
   - Shoulders
   - Arms
   - Hands or fists
   - Back
   - Upper legs
   - Lower legs
   - Feet

3. Now that you have squeezed and relaxed all your muscles, you should feel wiggly and limp like a noodle! Imagine you are limp and swaying from side to side, letting your arms dangle by your side and your hips sway. This is your Noodle Dance.

4. Continue to dance in a totally relaxed noodle way for a few minutes.

5. When you are done dancing, notice the calmness in your body.

> PLAY TIP: This is a great way for a younger child to work on visualization and relaxation by pretending to be a noodle. For older kids, you can use more body cues and still do the tensing and relaxing of different muscle groups but without the Noodle Dance.

Mountain Climbers

SUPPLIES: YOUR CHILD'S PREFERRED BODY LOTION

This is an adaptation of a popular Theraplay nurturing activity that involves positive touch between parent and child through the act of applying lotion. This adaptation incorporates firm touch to ground the child's emotions and is a fantastic technique to be used immediately prior to a stressful or challenging event when you need to bring your child's focus inward on self-regulation.

1. Discuss where on their body your child feels comfortable with you applying lotion. Arms work great for this activity, but legs, hands, and feet are also good options.

2. Warm up a quarter-size amount of lotion in your hands for a few moments.

3. When you are both ready, apply the lotion to the part of the body your child designated.

4. Now, using a light touch, pretend that your fingers are the legs of a mountain climber hiking up that part of your child's body. When the hiker reaches the top—whoops!—they lose their balance and slide down. This is done by gripping the body part and sliding your hands down while firmly squeezing. (The key here is the combination of the light touch crawling up the arm and the firm squeeze of sliding down.)

5. Continue for a few more rounds.

PLAY TIP: Some parents have found success in reducing opposition and defiance by incorporating this activity into their routines before an argument or disagreement would typically occur—for example, right before homework or immediately before the transition to bed—to get the child in a better headspace before the transition.

Butterfly Kisses

This activity continues to develop the mind–body connection and the ability to regulate and calm emotions through physical sensations and movements. It borrows bilateral stimulation techniques from eye movement desensitization and reprocessing (EMDR) therapy to calm the body. It also helps with development of skills related to processing and problem-solving because bilateral stimulation activates both hemispheres of the brain.

1. Stand facing each other with your arms outstretched and palms facing up.

2. Place your left hand across your chest to rest on the top of your right shoulder, and then place your right hand across your chest to the top of your left shoulder. You should be making a big X across your chest with both arms.

3. Now slowly tap each of your shoulders, alternating between left and right, so that you are tapping only one side at a time. It might be helpful to your child if you sing a song and you both tap to the beat. Great options are nursery rhymes or others with fifty-five to sixty-five beats per minute such as "Row, Row, Row Your Boat," "Baa, Baa, Black Sheep," and even "Stayin' Alive" by the Bee Gees.

4. Keep going at a slow to moderate pace for a couple minutes.

> PLAY TIP: An alternative to this activity is for you to do the alternate tapping for your child. You can try tapping their shoulders, knees, or hands while they are sitting in a chair. If your child is very sensitive to touch, you can have them track an item you hold back and forth with their eyes, making sure not to turn their head.

Tending My Garden

SUPPLIES: PAPER; COLORED PENCILS, CRAYONS, OR MARKERS

This self-control activity introduces your child to the importance of self-care and self-awareness and tending to our own internal needs so that we can better control our outward behaviors. Turns out it's a great metaphor for parents, too!

1. Draw a picture of a garden. It can be whatever type of garden you want but should include a few different plants. Don't color it in yet.

2. As you are drawing, think about what a garden needs to grow strong and healthy and discuss the needs with your partner. Things such as adequate sunshine, water, a gardener to tend to it, fertilizer, and a fence to keep out critters that would eat the plants are all examples. Add any of these things to your drawing.

3. Now imagine *you* as the garden. What do *you* need to grow? Who tends to your needs when you are not able to get them met on your own? What factors affect whether you are feeling your best? Think of needs you have for your physical body *and* for your emotional body. Discuss your needs with your partner.

4. Now add color to your drawing and hang your picture in a place you will see it often to remind yourself to take care of your own needs.

PLAY TIP: Just like putting on your own oxygen mask before assisting others in the event of an emergency on an airplane, as a parent you must take care of your own garden before you can tend to your child's garden. Modeling positive behaviors and self-care are some of the best ways to teach your child about self-control and self-awareness.

My Self-Control Ripple

SUPPLIES: PEN OR PENCIL

This activity is based on positive psychology and strengths-based approaches and focuses on the positive outcomes of using self-control. This exercise helps your child look outward beyond themselves and notice all the positives that come from responding to situations with self-control and helps point out the greater ripple effect of their positive behaviors.

1. Gently close your eyes and visualize a calm, still pond. The water is as smooth as glass.

2. Now imagine picking up a rock and throwing it far into the middle of the pond. You hear the *thunk* of the rock hitting the top of the water and sinking down to the bottom.

3. Visualize the spot where the rock hit the water. Imagine the ripples stemming out from the center.

4. Now imagine that self-control is the center of this ripple—the starting place of positive outcomes. Think about the good consequences or outcomes that occur when you use self-control.

5. Think of positive outcomes in each of these areas:

    a. Myself—positive outcomes you personally experience

    b. Family

    c. School or friends

    d. Neighborhood

    e. Greater society

6. Discuss the positive outcomes that came to mind. Use these examples to fill in the ripples on the next page.

> **PLAY TIP:** This page can be copied and hung in your child's room or any area of the house; it can be a great motivator and reminder to use self-control, as they will be seeing all the positive outcomes whenever they look at it!

CHAPTER FIVE

Solving Problems before They Get Out of Hand

THIS CHAPTER FOCUSES on the skills necessary for your child to engage in creative problem-solving. The first step in problem-solving is to have the insight to recognize that there is a problem and that we are a part of it in some way. The second step is the ability to use inhibition and restraint to halt the emotional response to the problem, followed by the next step of firing the most advanced and higher-functioning part of our brains to turn on critical thinking skills. Not an easy task!

To address the multitude of steps to effectively engage in problem-solving, these activities tackle skills related to cognitive challenging, reframing problems, and thinking of alternative or out-of-the-box solutions. They also highlight the need for structure to proactively solve problems as well as the importance of taking a step back when you are in the midst of a problem.

Calm Down Zone

OPTIONAL SUPPLIES: STUFFED ANIMALS, PILLOWS, LAMP, BOOKS, PAPER, PENCILS

This activity identifies the importance of designating an area of your home to be used when a family member needs a moment to think on their own away from the environment where the struggle is happening. This area is *not* to be used as a punishment or punitive measure, but as a proactive interference and positive opportunity for your child to pause, problem solve, and reset.

1. Think about your home and discuss your favorite place or room. Where do most of the fun family activities take place? In which part of your home do you spend the most time, and why?

2. Now think of an area your family can designate as the place where people go to take a moment to themselves to calm down. This area might be different for everyone or one place that everyone uses—it's up to each person to determine what works best for them.

3. Come up with a name for this area, or just call it the "Calm Down Zone." This is how you will refer to it when you are noticing a family member getting angry and you want to remind them that this area is available.

4. Think of items you would like to include in this area that will help you calm down so that you can problem solve or reset. Would it be nice to have soft or cuddly items in this space? Lighting? Books? Paper? If you can, gather these materials and bring them to this area so that it is ready to go.

> PLAY TIP: I cannot state strongly enough that sending your child to this area should *not* be used as a punishment. This area is to be framed as a positive time-out or pause so that everyone can reset and regroup and come back together when everyone is calm and has ideas for solving the problem.

Checklist to Calm

SUPPLIES: PAPER, PEN OR PENCIL, CRAYONS OR MARKERS (OPTIONAL)

Now that you have designated a Calm Down Zone (or whatever creative name you gave it), you and your child will create a checklist for the steps needed to use this space effectively. Making the checklist ahead of time allows for positive problem-solving when emotions are calm and peaceful rather than in a heated moment.

1. Discuss making a plan for how and when the Calm Down Zone will be used.

2. Together, create a checklist with categories in the following areas:

   • When should someone be asked to go to this area?

   • How will they know when they are calm and ready to leave?

   • What will happen when the person returns from the calm area?

3. When thinking of what to put on this checklist, remember to consider body language, tone of voice, and physical actions. For example:

   • Anytime someone in the family yells or uses an outside voice, they will be asked to take a moment in the Calm Down Zone.

   • That person will stay in the Calm Down Zone until their breathing is calm and steady.

   • When the family member returns, we will give one another a hug and then ask if they are better and want to try again.

4. Once your checklist is done, feel free to decorate it.

> **PLAY TIP:** Make a copy of this checklist and hang one in the Calm Down Zone and one in a common family area so that everyone can see it and direct one another to the area as needed.

Letter Search

SUPPLIES: ITEMS AROUND YOUR HOUSE

This activity focuses on strengthening problem-solving skills by tapping into the prefrontal cortex—the part of the brain that controls thinking, planning, and organizing. The more your child is able to tap into this part of their brain, the more regular this ability becomes and the more accessible it will be during an argument. This game is similar to a scavenger hunt but with a little twist.

1. Get ready to hunt for items that begin with a certain letter.

2. For the first round, use the letters in your child's name. For example, if your child's name is Marissa, you will need to find:

   - One item that begins with the letter M

   - Two items that begin with the letter A

   - One item that begins with the letter R

   - One item that begins with the letter I

   - Two items that begin with the letter S

3. For the second round, use your name. If that feels a little too easy, try finding items for your last name or both your first and last names during the same round.

4. The items do not have to be gathered. Just pointing them out works!

> PLAY TIP: It's okay to be creative and select an item based on its purpose. For example, a child may need to find an item for the letter G and select a red pen because it is used for grading. More creativity and problem-solving should be applauded!

Family Crossword

SUPPLIES: PAPER, PENCIL, RULER (OPTIONAL)

This brain teaser–type of activity also targets your child's prefrontal cortex somewhat. Creating a crossword puzzle incorporates problem-solving skills with creativity and planning, all great skills for a child with ODD to be able to tap into during a conflict.

1. Discuss what a crossword puzzle is, take a few moments to look at some together, and then complete a simple one for practice.

2. Now think of ten to twelve questions and answers for your own crossword puzzle. Try to use questions based on your family—for example, the name of your pet, a family member's favorite sports team, the street where you live, a common dish at mealtimes, and so on.

3. List the questions at the top of one piece of paper and the answers on another piece of paper.

4. Divide the list in half. One half will be for the words that go up and down, and one will be for words that go across. Number the up-and-down questions starting with 1 and the across questions starting with 1, too.

5. Now comes the hard part! Lay out your answers so that the letters of the answers intersect like in the crossword puzzle you did for practice. Try out different placements and spacing on scrap paper.

6. When you have the placement, draw rows and columns of boxes (a ruler is helpful here) to match your word arrangement, but only use the number of the question in the box where the word begins.

7. When you are done, give your crossword puzzle to another family member to see if they can solve it.

> PLAY TIP: Don't be alarmed if the puzzle creation is tough and you need to change some of your questions to get to an answer that fits the puzzle. This activity is all about problem-solving, and sometimes the solution is to be flexible and change the question!

Family Rules

SUPPLIES: POSTER BOARD OR PAPER, PEN OR MARKERS

For your child to be expected to engage in problem-solving to find positive alternatives to problems, they must first have a clear understanding of the expectations for behavior. Many families have unspoken rules that some members of the family may not fully comprehend or understand how to enforce. This activity can help solve this problem.

1. Gather all the family members together for this one! You will be creating family rules and will need everyone's input.

2. Discuss what rules each person thinks are important for families to follow—whether or not your family currently follows them.

3. Next, discuss things your family does well or each person's favorite part about your family.

4. Now merge these two discussions to make your family rules. These are clear guidelines or rules that *all* family members are expected to follow. Try to think of at least five family rules, covering areas such as how you will treat each other, how mealtimes will look, or even how the TV will be shared.

5. Write your family rules on the poster board or paper. Make sure they are written in clear and concise language. For example, avoid terms like "Use respectful language" as this can be confusing when it comes to application. Rules such as "We will use a calm voice when speaking to each other and allow each member to finish their sentence so they are not interrupted" is easier to enforce and understand.

> **PLAY TIP:** There is a time and a place for guidelines for your child's behavior to earn privileges (those are implemented later in addition to family rules to reinforce positive behavior), but this is not it! Family rules are for the family—not just for the youngest members.

My Routines

SUPPLIES: POSTER BOARD OR PAPER, MARKERS OR CRAYONS

Now that the family rules are set, it's time to problem solve the parts of the day that are typically the biggest struggle: the transitions needed for morning and bedtime routines. These parts of the day are often riddled with stress and a sense of panic that can lead to explosive arguments.

1. Discuss an ideal morning routine. Think about each family member's personality and temperament. For example, do some members hate the sense of being rushed? Does someone need additional time to change outfits until they find one that *feels* right?

2. Think about how these needs or strong desires can be accommodated, and work that into the morning routine (for example, waking up fifteen minutes earlier).

3. Now discuss the nighttime routine, taking into consideration what everyone needs.

4. Define when the nighttime routine will begin each evening. Then create the structure and timeline for each part of the routine. For example, determine about how much time each part of the routine needs and incorporate accordingly. When outlining the details, take into consideration realistic schedule conflicts—for example, do not schedule bath or shower time to start at 7:30 p.m. if soccer practice is on Wednesday nights and you don't get home until 8 p.m. The more consistency night by night, the better.

5. Write down the morning and nighttime routines on poster board or paper, decorate it, and hang it where it can be viewed in the morning and in the evening.

PLAY TIP: Allow your child to be a significant part of this process, but maintain control of the overall structure. This will help with motivation to follow the routines, and your mornings and evenings will likely go much more smoothly when everyone feels heard but within realistic limits.

My Life Raft

SUPPLIES: PEN OR PENCIL, CRAYONS OR COLORED PENCILS

This activity focuses on resources and supports needed to help your child solve problems. By proactively having these supports in place, you are setting up your child for success and increasing the likelihood they will be able to calmly tap into the prefrontal cortex and turn on their thinking brain in times of need.

1. Think about a life raft. What is its purpose? How is it used? When do we need one?

2. Discuss moments when you feel frustrated or angry or when things feel out of your control. What would it look like to have a life raft in these situations? A life raft can be anything that supports us when and if we need it to help us succeed. For example, during a hectic and stressful week, a hot shower or an extra twenty minutes of TV comedy time can be a life raft!

3. Help your child think about things that help them feel centered, calm, and in a better state of mind. Model some of your own life rafts to get your child's creative juices flowing if they are having a difficult time thinking about their own needs. On the next page, they can write these items in and around the life raft and decorate it, too.

> PLAY TIP: Just as your child needs a life raft every now and then, so do you! Make it a priority to support yourself as well. Peaceful households are not led by stressed-out parents. Problem solve what supports you in times of need so that you can continue to model desired behaviors for your child.

Tower of Power

SUPPLIES: BUILDING BLOCKS (NOT INTERLOCKING)

This game requires teamwork. You will be working together to engage in problem-solving to figure out how to build a bigger tower. Teamwork and talking through challenges are key skills for a child with ODD to develop to prevent challenges from turning into problems.

1. Stack the blocks in a single column and see how high you can build it before it falls over. Try this a few times and count how many blocks your tallest tower was before it fell.

2. Now take a moment to problem solve together. What does your tower need to break your record of the tallest one? What additional supports would be helpful to keep your tower from falling down?

3. After you have talked through a few different solutions and options, build another tower, but this time, it does not need to be one column. You can make it however you need to.

4. See if you are able to surpass your previous record. If so, talk about what helped and why.

PLAY TIP: Continue the conversation about your tower and how it needed a base or bigger supports to be successful. Turn it into a metaphor by asking your child about times when they needed a bigger base and what that means to them.

Toilet Paper Web

SUPPLIES: ROLL OF TOILET PAPER

This activity continues to engage your child's prefrontal cortex by requiring them to see the bigger picture and find creative additional ways a task can be done. This helps your child think of positive alternatives during an argument or new ways of seeing things by looking at the problem as a whole.

1. With the roll of toilet paper in hand, head to any room in your home you choose.

2. The idea is to make a web out of the toilet paper with as many crossover parts as you can. The more lines in your web, the better!

3. Find a spot to fasten one end of the toilet paper to and drape it to another anchor point and then to another anchor point, creating a web. Use your newly strengthened problem-solving skills to think of additional crossovers you can make and what in the room can serve as additional anchors to change directions. Think of ways to use your body to add more crossovers to your web, too. See if you can use the entire roll.

4. Talk with your partner about your strategy. Did you mostly move from one side of the room and then a long stretch all the way to the other side? Or did you focus on smaller, closer moves?

> PLAY TIP: For older kids, yarn is a great alternative material for this game. It can also be fun to do with the whole family so members can toss the yarn or toilet paper back and forth to each other to make the web.

How It's Made

SUPPLIES: YOUR CHILD'S FAVORITE ITEM OR TOY COMPOSED OF SEVERAL PIECES

This activity is a hands-on adaptation of the popular show by the same name. Using your child's favorite item will keep their engagement while firing those problem-solving regions of their brain. As a bonus, you get to connect with each other through talking about one of your child's areas of interest.

1. Look at the item or toy and comment on all the different pieces.

2. If you are able to do so carefully, take the item apart and separate it into the small pieces that make it. If you are not able to take the item apart, have your child examine it closely.

3. Talk about the different features and how the item is used. Are there parts of it that have different functions? How is this shown in the way it was designed? Are there ways to use it other than the original purpose?

4. Discuss how all of these parts and pieces work together.

5. As a team, return the item to its original state.

PLAY TIP: You might need to get the screwdriver out for this one, but let your child be the driving mechanic. During your conversation, use a metaphor about how situations in life need many different parts working in unison for things to work properly.

Picture Perfect

SUPPLIES: FORTY TO FIFTY SMALL ITEMS (SUCH AS BEADS, DRIED BEANS, CHEERIOS, OR CRAYONS)

This activity targets your child's prefrontal cortex by challenging their brain to help them focus on key details. This helps your child problem solve better by removing from their focus parts of the problem that are not important and allowing them to zero in on the details that matter.

1. Divide the pieces into two even groups, keeping one group for yourself and giving the other group to your child.

2. Use your items to create a design or picture of your choice; it could be lines, shapes, spirals, and so on.

3. Now have your child use their pieces to replicate your design. (Color doesn't matter in the case of multicolored pieces.)

4. Compare the images to see that they are identical, and then switch roles.

> **PLAY TIP:** If your child seems to do this fairly easily, add a challenge by having them make a mirror image of your design instead of a side-by-side replica. This will challenge their visualization and spatial-reasoning skills.

Hands Are for Kindness

SUPPLIES: PEN OR PENCIL, CRAYONS OR COLORED PENCILS

Physical aggression is often a big area of concern for parents of children with ODD, as it is the quickest route to social isolation and rejection by peers or siblings. This activity is meant to proactively reroute your child's brain to consider positive alternatives, thereby strengthening this pathway in their brain so that the behavior becomes more automatic.

1. Talk with your child about times their hands have gotten them in trouble. Physical aggression probably comes to mind first, but hands can also get us in trouble when we use them to grab items from other people or knock things over. Talk about some of the consequences that happen when we use unsafe hands.

2. Now discuss positive things your child can do with their hands instead. Great examples of kind hands include hugging, high fives, helping or assisting others, and tidying an area to make playing easier. Talk about how these behaviors could lead to good outcomes or positive consequences.

3. When your child has a few ideas for kind hands (how their hands will be used safely), they can write these ideas in the hands on the next page and decorate them, too.

> **PLAY TIP:** Help problem solve specific alternatives your child can do with their hands when they are frustrated or agitated that prevent them from hitting others—for example, squeezing and relaxing their fists, pushing their hands together in a prayer position, or flapping their hands at their side.

Kind Hands

Fever Pitch

SUPPLIES: ITEMS THAT ARE APPROPRIATE TO THROW

This activity focuses on problem-solving skills through identifying alternative appropriate choices. It specifically targets redirecting your child's behavior when they are angry and needing to find a physical outlet. Research shows that physical movement and outlets are great for children with ODD, and this activity directs that need in a positive direction.

1. Discuss with your child a time when they recently felt angry—so angry they wanted to throw or break something (and maybe they did). Talk about how sometimes being able to release anger in a physical way is helpful and give examples of times when you have felt this way, too.

2. Identify an alternative physical behavior that your child is allowed to engage in when they are angry and have a desire to throw something. Demonstrate small movements they can make with their hands or feet to try to diffuse the anger.

3. Now identify something silly or fun that can be thrown in lieu of something dangerous or breakable when they are angry so the same need or sensation of throwing is still being met. Some examples include throwing cotton balls, small pillows, and stuffed animals. If you are outside, a ball against a windowless brick wall works, too.

4. Practice throwing these approved items with your child and talk about directing them to do this the next time they feel angry.

> PLAY TIP: Throwing a soft item back and forth or throwing a ball outside together can turn this activity into a fun bonding moment. Use this time to model ways you cope with your anger and how you redirect yourself with distractions or other activities.

What Is a Compromise?

SUPPLIES: PAPER, PEN OR PENCIL

The purpose of this activity is to come up with definitions for complex terms so that everyone in the family is on the same page. Having clear definitions helps your child better understand the expectations around their behaviors so that they are more able to make positive choices during a disagreement or conflict. The key word for this activity is "compromise." You can switch it out for other words next time.

1. Talk with your child about what "compromise" means in your own words and give a few examples.

2. Now have your child describe the meaning of "compromise" in their own words.

3. Discuss times when you both successfully made a compromise, either with each other or with other people.

4. Write the word "compromise" in the middle of the paper. Then, working together, jot down as many examples as you can of what compromise looks like or means. This will help your child remember what you mean when you ask them to problem solve by figuring out a way to compromise.

5. Hang the "compromise" page where your child can see it daily to inspire them to make compromises!

PLAY TIP: The more you model compromises, the more your child will be willing to meet you in the middle. Having trouble with the bedtime routine? Model a compromise by allowing your child to choose which pajamas to wear that night.

Compromise This

SUPPLIES: PEN OR PENCIL

It's time to turn the new skill of compromising into problem-solving action! In this activity, your child will be presented with challenges that others are facing and asked to think of solutions that work as a compromise or positive outcome. Practicing this skill in moments of calm enables it to be better integrated and accessible for your child.

1. Discuss how we all need help sometimes. Often, when we are in the middle of a problem, we can't see all the possible solutions. It usually takes someone on the outside looking in to see the whole picture and come up with a plan that works for all.

2. Read the prompts on the next page. Write your solutions or compromises in the lines provided. The other person can use a separate piece of paper.

3. Think of outcomes that can help the most people or at least allow everyone to get their basic needs met—even if they don't get all their wishes met. Here's a tip: Put yourself in all the characters' positions and imagine if you would be satisfied with this solution if you were them.

4. Compare your answers and talk about any similarities.

> PLAY TIP: Take this activity up a notch by acting it out! Use some props to get into character and increase your child's sense of perspective-taking and empathy. Once they have acted out one perspective, switch and have them try the other point of view.

What's the Compromise?

Adrian gets easily irritated by his sister every day on the drive home from school. His sister seems to know exactly how to push his buttons and appears to enjoy getting his attention. Mom has said that if they fight in the car, they don't get TV later that day. How can they agree to get along so they both get what they want?

....

....

....

....

Marlo has many friends, but this time it's caused an issue for her! She has been invited to two birthday parties on the same day and can only attend one. One is for her long-term friend and is a smaller party. The other is for a newer friend at school who is having a big birthday bash. What should she decide?

....

....

....

....

Jacob and Mika both want to use the family iPad. Mom has told them that if they argue or fight, the iPad goes away. They both want to watch different shows, and usually this leads to a big, physical argument. What plan can they come up with that seems fair to both?

....

....

....

....

Friends to the Rescue

SUPPLIES: PAPER; PENCIL, CRAYONS, OR MARKERS

Now that your child has had the opportunity to be a friend to others in the previous activity by helping them come up with solutions, it's time to identify who comes to the rescue for them. This activity reminds your child that they are not alone and have many valuable resources to reach out to when they are feeling stuck.

1. Discuss how you and your child can turn to friends and trusted people for help when needed. Talk about how we all sometimes rely on others and point out that asking for help is a sign of strength, not weakness.

2. Help your child identify at least four to five people they can turn to for advice when their own problem-solving skills are not enough. Think of family elders, coaches, neighbors, teachers, or friends to help create their list of supporters.

3. Ask your child to draw a picture of each of these people, and while your child is drawing, talk about the characteristics of these people and why your child chose them as friends and trusted people to rely on.

> PLAY TIP: **After identifying these people with your child, talk with your child about ways they can be sure to have contact with each of these people regularly. Discuss how they can strengthen their relationships with them, and schedule activities or playdates accordingly!**

Snap List

SUPPLIES: POSTER BOARD OR PAPER, MARKERS

This activity focuses on using problem-solving to take kindness and helpfulness to the next level! You and your child will work together to think of some above-and-beyond behaviors, tasks, or chores and problem solve ways they can earn positive attention and praise from you for taking initiative to help a family member.

1. Describe your typical day to each other. What would make your day easier or run more smoothly? Focus on things you don't want the hassle of doing yourself or *always* doing yourself that are not part of your typical responsibilities at home.

2. When someone does one of these things for you or helps you with them, they earn "snaps" from you—praise, recognition, and thanks, along with a snap of your fingers and a smile.

3. Work together to identify eight to ten snaps for the family. Examples include helping a sibling with homework, organizing a messy closet or family drawer, and raking leaves in the yard. Snaps are not typically given for someone taking care of their own responsibilities, but a family member would typically get snaps for helping someone with their responsibilities after they have taken care of their own.

4. Make a list of the behaviors that earn snaps on the poster board or paper to create a family "Snap List" and display it somewhere for everyone to see.

> **PLAY TIP:** Decide together how family members will be recognized for earning snaps to encourage these behaviors. Positive attention is one of the most effective means of reinforcement for children and does not cost you a penny!

My Proud Moments

SUPPLIES: PAPER; PEN, PENCIL, CRAYONS, OR MARKERS

This activity follows up "Snap List" (page 111) with more focus on catching your child doing things right and giving praise and positive attention when warranted. The more energy and attention you put toward your child's positive behaviors, the more those pathways in your child's brain will be strengthened and reinforced!

1. Ask your child to think of moments when they felt proud. Talk through some examples together and offer your own insights on days you felt really proud and encouraged by their behavior, too.

2. Continue this conversation by identifying some of your child's strengths and the problem-solving skills they are using. For example, did they recently show flexibility when a friend wanted to play a different game and they went along with it? Did they accept the news calmly when the baseball game was canceled due to rain? These are great examples of successful problem-solving skills.

3. Ask your child to write a story or draw a picture of some of their strengths or successes to give more emphasis to their successes. While they are drawing, offer encouragement by talking about the positive outcomes you have witnessed when they engaged in problem-solving.

> **PLAY TIP:** When coupled with clear examples, words of encouragement mean the most and are integrated into your child's self-concept. Be concrete when talking about your child's successes and provide examples while giving praise.

Problem Tank

SUPPLIES: BOX OR JAR, STRIPS OF PAPER, PEN OR PENCIL

In this activity, which can be done with the whole family, your child will be using their problem-solving skills to find solutions to various family conflicts. The key to this is that the problem-solving is done during a calm time when the thinking part of the brain can be accessed (rather than in the heat of the moment).

1. Have each family member think of a recent conflict they had with another family member. These can be one-time conflicts, but regular conflicts work best for this activity—for example, conflicts around homework time or bedtime.

2. Each family member writes a brief description of the conflict they thought of on a strip of paper. They can do this for more than one conflict if there are others they also thought of.

3. Fold the strips of paper and put them in the jar or box. This is now your Problem Tank! The Problem Tank holds the conflicts until you are ready to calmly work through them together.

4. Schedule a time each week for the family to come together, withdraw one strip of paper to read out loud, and use problem-solving skills to come up with a solution or new plan to try to eliminate this family conflict. If the conflict has not been occurring lately or has already been solved, take out another conflict and work on solving that one.

> **PLAY TIP:** Family members can place additional conflicts in the Problem Tank as they occur. This way, you will always have challenges to work through together. Even if the conflicts seem small, the important part is that the family comes together to work on solving problems.

Turn It Around

This activity focuses on the therapeutic skill of cognitive reframing, looking at something in a new way. Your child will be challenged to use their strengthened problem-solving skills to reframe negative statements in a positive way, firing those neurons more in the direction of resourcefulness and positive solutions.

1. Discuss the concept of reframing: turning negative statements into positive statements. To reframe something means to look at it in a new or different way that hasn't been considered yet.

2. Talk about how sometimes, when we are in the middle of a problem, it is difficult to reframe it or to think of solutions. Taking a few minutes or even hours to step away from the problem can often help with our ability to reframe the situation and come back with positive solutions.

3. Read the statements on the next page with your child, and encourage them to use their creativity and problem-solving skills to rewrite the statements into positive statements. Here's an example:

   • Negative statement: *Maya spent so much time working on her homework that she was unable to watch any TV before dinner.*

   • Positive reframing: *Maya worked very hard on her homework, put in her best effort. and got it all completed.*

Turn Negatives into Positives

Colette dropped her ice cream, and it got all over the floor, so she had to help her dad clean it up.

Reframe positively:

_____

_____

_____

George's team lost their soccer game in the final minute when the other team scored from a penalty kick.

Reframe positively:

_____

_____

_____

Nikki doesn't like one of the foods Mom made for dinner and feels like she never gets to eat what she likes.

Reframe positively:

_____

_____

Julian hates it when his little brother tags along with him to playdates because his friends seem to be more interested in his brother than in him.

Reframe positively:

_____

_____

_____

CHAPTER SIX

Building Connections and Self-Esteem

WELCOME TO THE last set of activities! By now, you have likely seen a decrease of ODD symptoms in your child from using this workbook together. Let's finish up by directly targeting your parent–child relationship.

Children with ODD are often identified as the difficult or challenging members of the family and tend to be in trouble. These activities focus on creating stronger positive connections with your child to improve their self-esteem and internalized feelings about themselves. The better a child feels about themselves on the inside, the better their outward behavior. With these activities, you will have opportunities to engage in connection-building moments of fun and laughter while also increasing your child's self-esteem by identifying their strengths and successes. You will also model how to engage in self-care and self-compassion.

What Is Self-Esteem?

Helping your child develop positive self-esteem gives them a strong foundation for improved behavior. When your child feels more positively about themselves, your relationship with your child has the opportunity to grow and strengthen. But they must first understand the concept of self-esteem.

1. Discuss the definition of "self-esteem" in as few words as possible so that it is easy for all family members to understand.

2. Talk about things that can increase a person's sense of self-esteem. Offer examples of your own that have increased your overall opinion of yourself, and then offer examples of what you think may have enhanced your child's self-esteem.

3. Next, discuss what might decrease someone's self-esteem, such as moments of rejection or perceived abandonment. Talk about some of the behaviors people engage in that might lead to a decrease in self-esteem and brainstorm ways to avoid these.

4. With a better understanding of what self-esteem means for your family, discuss how you might all incorporate small daily tasks to increase the self-esteem of everyone in the family.

> **PLAY TIP:** For younger children, abstract concepts such as self-esteem are more difficult to understand. Make sure your definition uses the child's own language so they can better grasp the concept, such as "Self-esteem is how happy or sad we feel about ourselves."

What I Like about Me

SUPPLIES: PAPER; COLORED PENCILS, MARKERS, OR CRAYONS

This self-esteem-building activity helps your child turn inward to identify things they like about themselves. We all know it feels good to receive compliments from others, but the effects are far stronger if the compliment comes from within and your child is able to identify their own positives. Your child will be working to identify what they like most about themselves; your job is to help them with this without offering your own comments and compliments—yet! That activity comes later.

1. Ask your child to draw a self-portrait or, if they prefer, to engage in free or abstract drawing instead. The key here is for their hands to be busy to free up their mind a bit to think about positive things about themselves.

2. As they are drawing, ask your child to name some of their favorite characteristics about themselves. Encourage them to identify at least three to five characteristics that make them feel good about themselves.

3. Your child can write these characteristics around their self-portrait or other design so that in moments of self-doubt they can look at this drawing.

PLAY TIP: If your child struggles to identify their favorite characteristics about themselves, you can guide them to certain topics without leading too much. Certain prompts, such as thinking about what makes them feel good about themselves when they are with friends or what they are passionate about, can help get the wheels turning.

In My Heart, Part Two

SUPPLIES: PEN, PENCIL, CRAYONS, OR COLORED PENCILS

The activities in this category focus on creating stronger connections and positive bonds between you and your child as well as with all the other special people in your child's life. In the activity "In My Heart" on page 24, your child identified *things* that make them feel loved. Along those lines, your child will now identify the special *people* who have a positive impact on them and on whom they can count to help them feel better about themselves.

1. Ask your child to think about the positive people in their life—the people they trust and who help them feel loved, valued, and important. Who are they?

2. Discuss why it is important to have people like this in their life and how they feel during interactions with these people. Focusing on how your child feels during interactions with these people will help your child develop internal motivation to cultivate and strengthen these relationships. Talk about how positive relationships increase our self-esteem and sense of self-worth.

3. Ask your child to write the names of these people or draw pictures of them in the heart on the next page.

PLAY TIP: This activity helps children realize that self-esteem is grown both through relationships with others and with themselves. The discussion in this activity focuses on the former and how positive interactions with others ultimately enable us to feel better about ourselves.

This Is Who Is in My Heart

Secret Code Word

This and the next few activities focus on increasing the positive connection between you and your child. For this activity, you will create a secret code word together that only the two of you know. This creates frequent opportunities for shared laughter and connection because you are the only ones in on the secret!

1. Discuss what your secret code word will be. Get as silly as you want! Made-up words work well, too!

2. Next, decide what your secret code word will mean. For instance, is it a greeting you use to say hello or goodbye? Is it a word you say when you want to let the other person know you love them? Or is it something you say instead of rolling your eyes when someone is doing something silly? Your secret code word can mean anything you want it to.

3. Strengthen your bond by each coming up with a few scenarios throughout the day when you can use your secret code word.

> **PLAY TIP:** Continued use of your secret code word will help create moments of laughter and add lightness to your day. This is also a fun way to make other family members really curious! Play up the uniqueness of this secret code word by using it out in public to make your child feel really special.

Forehead Frenzy

SUPPLIES: DECK OF PLAYING CARDS (JOKERS REMOVED)

This game is a fun way to strengthen your connection with your child and bring more joy to your parent–child relationship. This game is similar to one I grew up playing as a child, but it incorporates more of a challenge and therefore requires more communication and connection to get the answer.

1. Decide who will go first. The first player shuffles or mixes the deck of cards. Without looking (or peeking!) at it, they pick a card and hold it face out on their forehead so that the second player can see what it is.

2. The first player now asks the second player a series of yes-or-no questions to figure out which card they are holding. For instance, "Is it black?" and "Is it a face card?" The first player continues asking yes-or-no questions until they are able to correctly guess the card.

3. Switch roles for another round.

> **PLAY TIP:** Increase the challenge by limiting the number of yes-or-no questions that can be asked per round. To simplify for younger children, start by trying to guess just the number or face on the card; once they get the hang of it, they can try to guess the number or face and the suit.

Squiggle Game

SUPPLIES: PAPER, CRAYONS OR MARKERS

This activity is intended to increase the parent–child connection and requires flexibility, patience, and cooperation—all wonderful skills to target for a child with ODD. This is a simple activity you can even do at restaurants while waiting for the food to arrive if you bring along the supplies. You, the parent, should be the first player in order to demonstrate the game when starting out.

1. Each player selects a marker or crayon of a different color.

2. The first person draws a squiggle on the paper using their color in one consecutive line. It can be as long or as short as you want. As soon as the crayon or marker leaves the paper, the squiggle is done.

3. Hand the paper to the other player, whose role it is to turn the squiggle into a picture using their color.

4. When done, the other player tells a story about the picture they created from the squiggle.

5. Switch roles and play again.

> PLAY TIP: Up the ante by passing the paper back and forth a few times. One person creates the squiggle (you, the first time to illustrate), and then the other person adds a few lines to the picture and passes it back. Trade the paper every ten to fifteen seconds until you both decide the drawing is complete.

Xs and Os

SUPPLIES: PAPER, SCISSORS, MARKERS, TAPE

Positive physical touch is the fastest way to calm a child's brain and can also be used when you notice your child's emotions building and you need a quick way to calm them down. This activity identifies the manner in which your child is comfortable engaging in physical connection and contact with you.

1. Draw two horizontal lines and one vertical line on your piece paper, dividing it into six parts. Draw an X inside three of the squares and an O inside the other three squares.

2. Cut out the squares so that each person has six squares total (three Xs and three Os).

3. Discuss how each of you likes to show affection or love with a family member and how you like to receive this love. Talk about whether you prefer giving hugs and kisses or if high fives or fist bumps are more your thing.

4. Decide together what the Xs and Os represent. For example, in some families, Xs represent kisses, and Os represent hugs. Each family is different, and you may decide that hugs are Os, but Xs represent hand squeezes.

5. Tape the Xs and Os on your body to show the other person where you feel comfortable receiving physical contact and in what way.

6. Practice giving each other physical affection based on the meaning and placement of the other person's Xs and Os.

> **PLAY TIP:** This is a wonderful way to begin teaching your child how to set boundaries with their body and express ways they are comfortable receiving physical attention or contact from you. It's important to follow your child's boundaries and refrain from kissing or other contact if they express that they're not comfortable with receiving that type of affection.

The Calm Home

SUPPLIES: PEN, COLORED PENCILS, OR CRAYONS

This activity continues the theme from "Safe Zone" (page 22) but places emphasis on what each family member says or does that helps the home feel peaceful. When you focus on how each person contributes in their own unique way to the sense of safety and calmness in the home, the parent–child connection strengthens.

1. Discuss what makes a home feel calm or safe.

2. Work together to identify what each family member does to add to this sense of calmness in the home. Identifying each family member's strengths may help. For example, if one parent's strength is to remain calm during an argument (the least likely to yell), their special role in creating calmness is to take over during an argument while the other parent takes a breather. One sibling's strength may be using humor, which can be a great distraction during an argument because they make everyone laugh with their antics.

3. On the next page, as you discuss the special role each family member plays to bring calmness and peacefulness to the home, ask your child to draw a picture of it or write it in the house.

> PLAY TIP: Giving your attention to what you want instead of what you don't want is the law of attraction in play. Even if your house never feels calm or peaceful, focusing on what *would* make it feel calm points you in the right direction.

Our Calm Home

Note to Self

SUPPLIES: PAPER, PEN OR PENCIL

This activity touches on the importance of self-compassion and self-love as part of a child's overall self-esteem by having them focus on the important things in their life that they want to remember years from now. Arguments might feel big in the moment, but this activity helps your child focus on the bigger, more valuable moments filled with love and connection.

1. Think about the important or big moments in your life that have happened recently. Think of your successes and things you feel proud of that you want to remember in the future so you can give yourself a pat on the back.

2. Now imagine yourself ten years in the future. With that image in mind, write your future self a letter.

3. Write about your successes and the things you are proud of, but also describe moments when you felt the most loved, important, heard, or included. These are the moments to cherish because they make everything worthwhile.

4. Make your letter as long as you like, and when you're done, sign it.

> PLAY TIP: In your own letter, as the parent, be sure to include notes to yourself about special moments in your relationship with your child and read it after particularly hard days. It can help you remember the love and connection you also share.

Worthy of the News

SUPPLIES: PAPER, PEN OR PENCIL, CLOTHING PROPS (OPTIONAL)

This activity places attention on one particular success or accomplishment your child has had recently so that you can really celebrate this success. This activity strengthens the positive connection between you and your child by continuing to focus on good parts of the relationship and taking energy away from the conflict and opposition.

1. Pretend that you are both news reporters, investigating the other person's recent success.

2. Write a short segment for the evening news, focusing on that success. For example, you will focus on something your child did exceptionally well recently. It can be something as simple as making their bed that morning or something big like performing in the school talent show. Your child can choose something about you that they think would make a positive, newsworthy story. For example, perhaps you recently helped them organize all their toys or received a compliment from your boss at work.

3. When your news segments are ready, take turns acting as if you are reporters on the evening news. Use props if you'd like.

PLAY TIP: You can make this activity more fun and humorous by seeing who can have the most exaggerated announcer's voice. To make it more playful for younger children, you can also use silly statements like "And now on location . . ." or "Back to you in the studio!"

Written in the Sand

SUPPLIES: DRY-ERASE BOARD, MARKERS, ERASER

This activity teaches some coping skills and management techniques by first identifying something challenging or upsetting and then practicing letting it go. Activities such as this one can create more closeness and connection in your parent–child relationship through vulnerability and the ability to comfort and validate each other.

1. Think of one of your burdens—something that is hard or challenging or makes you feel sad or upset. Talk with the other person about this difficulty or challenge and why it makes you feel sad or upset.

2. Write a few words about that challenge on the dry-erase board and then wipe it away and tell it goodbye! You are letting it go.

3. Talk with the other person about how much better it feels to not have to carry this challenge around with you anymore.

4. Take turns writing and erasing things you are letting go of, including conflict or irritants in your parent–child relationship and other things you are able to move past.

> PLAY TIP: If you don't have a dry-erase board, a steamy bathroom mirror or shaving cream work, too. Trace the words with your finger in the shaving cream or on the foggy mirror and then wipe the words away. Weather permitting, you can do this activity in wet sand or a little patch of dirt; write the words with a stick or even your fingers, and then wipe them away with your hands.

High Five

SUPPLIES: PAPER, MARKERS OR CRAYONS

This activity creates a loving moment of connection through identifying positives about each other. It also incorporates a little bit of safe and comforting positive touch through tracing the hand to increase the connection and sense of closeness. Last, this activity gives your child an opportunity to praise you and acknowledge some of your talents and strengths.

1. Trace outlines of each other's hands onto separate pieces of paper. Be sure to spread your fingers wide so there is room for the marker to make its way around each finger.

2. In the outline of the other person's hand, list one positive attribute or characteristic about that person in each of the five fingers.

3. When you are done, decorate the pictures and exchange them as gifts of gratitude.

PLAY TIP: For older children, write a few words about what you admire about the other person in each finger—for example, "You give the best hugs when I am sad" and "Your sense of humor makes me laugh."

I Am...

SUPPLIES: PEN OR PENCIL, CRAYONS OR COLORED PENCILS (OPTIONAL)

This activity continues to build your child's self-esteem by identifying more of your child's positive personality traits and characteristics. This is a great opportunity for your child to gain insight and awareness of the skills they already possess and can share with the world in a positive manner.

1. The prompts on the next page are intended to bring to light positive strengths and attributes your child already possesses but perhaps doesn't always take the time to acknowledge and remember.

2. Ask your child to complete each of these statements in their own words, focusing on creating positive statements. This helps you and your child reframe and think about their behaviors in a new light, perhaps by viewing certain traits as strengths rather than as challenges.

3. Your child can decorate and color the page when they are done if they would like and look at it for encouragement throughout the week.

> PLAY TIP: Take this activity a step further by having your child choose a few of these statements to use as positive affirmations that they can repeat to themselves throughout the day. You can also create a moment of connection by saying the affirmations together a few times when your child needs some encouragement.

I Am . . .

I am taller than a tree when ....

....

I am stronger than a bear when ....

....

I am as playful as a dolphin when ....

....

I am more determined than the tides when ....

....

I am brighter than the sun when ....

....

I am as steadfast as the sea when ....

....

I am as peaceful as a breeze when ....

....

I am brave like a lion when ....

....

Calm Touches

This activity incorporates some of the latest brain research that shows safe, comforting physical touch is the fastest way to reach a child's brain to tap into the self-calming and self-regulating regions. This is similar to "Friendly Feather Tickles" (page 53) and "Xs and Os" (page 125), which focus on where your child feels safe being touched, but the key for this activity is the *type* of touch they prefer.

1. Discuss how everyone has a preferred mode or method of touch that feels good to them. Explain that it is important to clearly communicate this preference to each other so that the touch you share is soothing and calming. (To create a positive connection, it should not feel forced or uncomfortable.)

2. Ask questions to determine what type of touch your child likes. Do they like firm or soft touch? Quick taps or prolonged squeezes? Once you have narrowed it down, practice this type of touch to strengthen your bond and connection.

3. To make it playful, give this type of touch a fun name. For example, if your child enjoys prolonged, firm hugs or squeezes, you can name these something like "bear hugs" or "Hulk hugs." If they prefer brief hand squeezes, you might name these "strong hands" or "fist squeezies." Work together to make the name your own.

> PLAY TIP: Incorporate this calm touch into regular moments throughout your child's day. A great way to prevent struggles is to give this calm touch before the time when a struggle typically occurs, such as giving it right when they wake up if they struggle with the transition out of bed in the morning.

Back-to-Back Sharing

Ever notice how your child often gives you a one-word response when you ask about their day, but when you are lying beside them at bedtime, they don't stop talking? This phenomenon occurs because it is generally easier to be vulnerable when we aren't face-to-face with someone or looking them in the eyes to see their reaction—or allowing them to see ours. This activity targets this phenomenon and incorporates some positive physical touch. Notice how much more communication you are able to get when face-to-face contact isn't forced.

1. Sit on the floor cross-legged in opposite directions. Scoot closer until your backs are touching.

2. Share a recent positive memory or experience you had with your child. This allows your child to share in this moment without feeling too vulnerable, as if they need to respond, or that you will be looking at their facial reaction—and vice versa.

3. Now it your child's turn to share a recent positive memory or experience they had with you.

4. Do a few rounds of back-to-back sharing to deepen your connection and mutual joy.

> PLAY TIP: If your child tends to vent at bedtime, do this activity in the early evening and encourage them to share whatever is on their mind (instead of just positive experiences) to help reduce their need to process their day out loud at bedtime.

How We Roll

SUPPLIES: DIE OR COIN

This activity targets both self-esteem and connection through joyful exercises and shared moments that also make your child feel good in their body and therefore good about themselves. The prompts here are all geared toward bringing more joy to your parent–child relationship or calming your child's nervous system when life feels hectic. It's also a great break from busy schedules to focus on being together and creating more calmness.

1. Turn to the next page, and place the workbook flat.

2. Take turns rolling the die or flipping the coin to land on one of the activities. When it is your turn, do the activity the die or coin lands on. If it touches more than one space, it is your choice.

3. Continue until you have had a chance to do a few activities each.

> PLAY TIP: You can also do all six activities together in whatever order feels best to you. Remember, your child's self-esteem builds when they listen to themselves and engage in behaviors that make them feel better or good; therefore, if none of these activities resonates, ask them to create their own six activities. As long as they are safe and create joy and connection, they're good!

How We Roll Activities

1 Do any stretch that feels good to your body.

2 Tell your favorite joke.

3 Take three deep breaths.

4 Shake your sillies out! Shake your whole body for ten seconds.

5 Share a success you had today and ask the other person to give you a standing ovation!

6 Give each other a hug or engage in your calm touch with each other.

Star Player

SUPPLIES: PAPER; INDEX CARDS; PENCIL, CRAYONS, OR MARKERS

This is your child's opportunity to be the MVP of the family! This activity is intended to increase joy and connection in your parent–child relationship by celebrating family members and giving your child a chance to feel like a star or an important and valued part of the family—as opposed to a source of conflict or challenges.

1. Write the words "Star Player" at the top of the paper. Write the name of each family member on an index card.

2. As your child decorates the Star Player page (leaving blank space at the bottom third on which to tape one of the notecards), discuss what qualifies someone as the Star Player of the family for a day. Talk about how this title can be earned by going the extra mile to help someone out or by accomplishing something—for example, scoring points in the basketball game, getting homework done on time, or clearing their plate from the table without being asked.

3. Once you have discussed what will earn someone this title, assign the first Star Player! Choose from among the index cards and tape that person's name to the bottom of the page. Hang this where the whole family can see it.

4. Each day, assign a new Star Player by removing the index card and taping up the next Star Player's name.

PLAY TIP: Keep in mind that accomplishments and successes are relative. For example, if your child typically earns C grades, earning a B on an assignment would be worthy of being named Star Player for the day! This helps keep your focus on appropriate expectations for each child.

Common Ground

SUPPLIES: PAPER, PEN OR PENCIL

This and the next few activities place a lot of emphasis on building closeness and connection between you and your child. This activity centers on finding commonalities and shared interests. Talking about what you and your child have in common can help you feel as if you are on the same team instead of constantly butting heads.

1. Discuss how people often share interests and may like and dislike (or simply prefer) the same things as someone else. This is common ground.

2. Now list as many things as you can about the other person that you think you both have in common. Think about your interests and preferences in various subjects and topics—for example, food and sports. You can also think of preferences such as for the beach over mountains, hot weather versus cold, sweet smells over earthy smells, quiet sounds over loud sounds, being in large groups over alone time, trying new things over sticking with what you know and love, and so on.

3. Compare your list of commonalities and shared preferences and, together, create one master list.

4. Put a star next to the top three you both feel the most strongly about.

PLAY TIP: Make reference to your commonalities and shared preferences throughout the day to create moments of connection with your child. For example, around dinnertime, you can comment that tonight you are having broccoli with dinner "because it is our favorite vegetable!"

We Rise Up

SUPPLIES: PAPER, CRAYONS OR MARKERS

This activity was inspired by former First Lady Michelle Obama and her directive for us all to rise up instead of stooping down to other people's levels when they engage in negative behaviors. This is a great affirmation for children with ODD because it reminds them that we can always choose to engage in positive behaviors that lead to better outcomes for all.

1. Discuss with your child what it means to stoop down to someone else's level—that is, to respond to someone's negative or unkind behavior with similar negative or unkind behavior. Talk about how we are often inclined to engage in this type of behavior when we want someone to feel as hurt and as rejected as we are feeling as a result of their words or actions.

2. Now talk about what it means to rise up and the different outcomes that occur as a result.

3. Discuss the obstacles and difficulties in rising up and how this takes active intention and practice to become second nature. Come up with a few solutions to avoid or overcome what might get in the way of rising up.

4. Ask your child how they can rise up to family members, siblings, friends, school, their community, and the greater population, offering guidance as needed.

5. Ask your child to write some of the reminders or tips for rising up on paper and decorate it with drawings of them rising up and helping others.

> **PLAY TIP:** Using this "rise up" language when talking to your child after arguments or conflicts can help them integrate this method of behavior more strongly in their brain. During conflicts at home, see if you can pause and talk through together how you can both rise up in that exact moment to stop the conflict in its path.

Fill My Bucket

SUPPLIES: JAR OR BOX, PAPER, SCISSORS, PEN OR PENCIL

This activity is taken from a much-loved book of a similar name, *How Full Is Your Bucket?* by Tom Rath and Mary Reckmeyer. In this activity, your child will focus on finding ways to fill their bucket—that is, engage in behaviors that increase their sense of well-being, spanning the areas of physical, social, and emotional health.

1. Place the jar or box in a place you will see it often. This will be your child's "bucket"—a physical representation of all the kind and helpful behaviors and comments they make throughout the week.

2. Cut the paper into small strips and place the strips near the bucket along with a pen or pencil.

3. Throughout the week, notice the helpful or kind things your child does. If you are out, verbalize it to your child and remind them that this behavior will fill their bucket. Write it down and put it in their bucket as soon as you get home. If you are at home when the positive behavior occurs, stop what you are doing, praise your child, write it down, and put the strip into their bucket.

4. Decide how you will celebrate your child when their bucket is full. Ideas include choosing the movie for a family movie night, selecting dessert that week, or picking a fun family weekend activity.

> PLAY TIP: Your child can receive recognition for positive self-care behaviors as well as positive behaviors toward others. The act of writing down these positive acts and putting them into the bucket helps rewire your child's brain toward making positive choices and strengthens this habit.

Resources

PARENTING BOOKS

No-Drama Discipline: The Whole-Brain Way to Calm the Chaos and Nurture Your Child's Developing Mind by Daniel J. Siegel, MD, and Tina Payne Bryson, PhD (Bantam Books, 2016)
A book focused on connecting brain development with parental techniques for responding to misbehavior in a compassionate and positive way.

The Whole-Brain Child: 12 Revolutionary Strategies to Nurture Your Child's Developing Mind by Daniel J. Siegel, MD, and Tina Payne Bryson, PhD (Bantam Books, 2012)
This book provides an approach to parenting that fosters healthy brain development and aids in raising calmer, happier children.

CHILDREN'S BOOKS

I Am Human: A Book of Empathy by Susan Verde (Abrams Books, 2018)
A wonderful book for children first grasping the definition of empathy and its impact and power to shape their interactions with others.

The Invisible Web: A Story Celebrating Love and Universal Connection by Patrice Karst (Little, Brown and Company, 2020)
This is a classic therapy office book, along with its sister book, *The Invisible String*, which enables children to feel their parents' love and connection despite long distances.

WEBSITES

Center on the Developing Child, Harvard University (developingchild.harvard.edu)
This is a free platform for science-based innovation and research to achieve a promising future for every child.

Parenting Science (parentingscience.com)
Parenting Science offers free resources and information for parents, covering many phases of child development and well-being.

Parenting: The New York Times (nytimes.com/section/parenting)
Cutting-edge parenting articles covering a wide range of topics and current events. Many articles specifically address the common struggles of parenting and offer tips on how to navigate parenting difficulties and hardships.

TODAY Parenting Guides, in Collaboration with Chan Zuckerberg Initiative (today.com/parenting-guides)
TODAY Parenting Guides provide benchmarks and tips for children's academic, physical, and social emotional growth.

PODCASTS

The Brain Architects by the Center on the Developing Child at Harvard University (developingchild.harvard.edu/collective-change/communicating-the-science/the-brain-architects-podcast)
The Brain Architects offers research- and science-based podcasts and resources on child development, including podcasts related to the psychological effects of the COVID-19 pandemic on children.

Message from Mom by Whitney Rowell (chartable.com/podcasts/message-from-mom)
Message from Mom provides resources for moms on all aspects of parenting and personal development.

Raising Good Humans by Dr. Aliza Pressman (draliza.com)
Developmental psychologist and co-founder of Mount Sinai Parenting Center Dr. Aliza Pressman creates thoughtful and entertaining parenting podcasts to perk up your morning drive to work.

References

American Psychiatric Association. *Diagnostic and Statistical Manual of Mental Disorders Fifth Edition Text Revision (DSM-5-TR).* Washington, DC: American Psychiatric Association Publishing, 2022.

Chapman, Gary, and Ross Campbell. *The 5 Love Languages of Children: The Secret to Loving Children Effectively.* Chicago: Northfield Publishing, 1997.

Crisci, Geraldine, Marilyn Lay, and Liana Lowenstein. *Paper Dolls and Paper Airplanes: Therapeutic Exercises for Sexually Traumatized Children.* Minneapolis, MN: Jist Works, 1998.

EMDR Institute, Inc. "Welcome to EMDR.com." Accessed May 3, 2022. emdr.com.

Grulon Paz, Isabella. "Full Transcript of Michelle Obama's D.N.C. Speech." *The New York Times.* August 17, 2020. nytimes.com/2020/08/17/us/politics/Michelle-Obama-speech-transcript-video.html.

Keltner, Dacher. "Hands On Research: The Science of Touch." Greater Good Magazine. September 29, 2010. greatergood.berkeley.edu/article/item/hands_on_research.

Kilner, J. M., and R. N. Lemon. "What We Know Currently about Mirror Neurons." *Current Biology* 23, no. 23 (December 2013): R1057–R1062. doi.org/10.1016/j.cub.2013.10.051.

Rath, Tom, and Mary Reckmeyer. *How Full Is Your Bucket? For Kids.* New York: Gallup Press, 2009.

Strøm, Vegard, Marita S. Fønhus, Eilin Ekeland, and Gro Jamtvedt. "Physical Exercise for Oppositional Defiant Disorder and Conduct Disorder in Children and Adolescents." *Cochrane Database of Systemic Reviews* 2017, no. 1 (January 2017): CD010670. doi.org/10.1002/14651858.CD010670.pub2.

The Theraplay Institute. "The Theraplay Institute." Accessed May 3, 2022. theraplay.org.

University of Pennsylvania, School of Arts and Sciences. "Positive Psychology Center." Accessed May 3, 2022. ppc.sas.upenn.edu.

Wikipedia. "Stanford Marshmallow Experiment." Accessed May 3, 2022. en.wikipedia.org/wiki/Stanford_marshmallow_experiment.

Index

Acknowledgments

I would like to first acknowledge Vanessa Putt with Callisto Media for bringing this project to my attention and helping bring it to fruition. Thank you to my editor, Chloe Moffett, and the team at Rockridge Press for guiding me through my first book project with patience and grace.

Thank you to my friends and family for your patience and support during the writing process and allowing the writing to take a priority for a duration of time. Thank you to my professional colleagues and employees at HeadFirst Counseling. You all inspire me each and every day with your outstanding clinical skills.

Thank you to my husband for your unwavering support in all my endeavors. And to my son—you are my raison d'être.

About the Author

LAURA McLAUGHLIN, LPC SUPERVISOR, RPT, is a registered play therapist and licensed professional counselor based in Dallas, Texas. She is the founder of HeadFirst Counseling, a private practice therapy group in Dallas where she specializes in treating ADHD, oppositional and defiant behaviors, emotional dysregulation, sensory sensitivities, trauma, and high-functioning autism spectrum disorders in children. Laura attended the University of Texas at Austin for her undergraduate degree and received her master of education in counseling degree from the University of North Texas with a specialization in play therapy.

Immediately following graduate school, Laura had a brief stint living in New York City and worked at the Child Mind Institute before returning to Dallas. Prior to going into private practice, Laura worked for local nonprofit agencies, including The Family Place and the Dallas Children's Advocacy Center, providing therapy services to child survivors of domestic violence and sexual abuse. For more information, visit headfirstdallas.com.

CPSIA information can be obtained
at www.ICGtesting.com
Printed in the USA
JSHW062143051122
32609JS00001B/1